Dimple Dares to Dream

Story by

Bola Dada

THIS BOOK BELONGS TO

_____

First published in the United Kingdom in 2025

© 2025 by Bola Dada

Email: adebola.dada1@outlook.com

British Library Cataloguing in Publication Data
A CIP catalogue record for this book is available from the British Library.

ISBN: 9-781739-098995

Editorial and Publishing services by The Heritage Publishers Limited
Cover design by Hatice Bayramoglu

Printed in the United Kingdom

PREFACE

> ✼ ‹

With many writers focusing on books for young children or adults, there is a gap in the reading material available to children in their teens. I focus on writing for children in their early teenage years so they can be inspired to continue reading.

My first book, *Dimple Dares to Ask*, recollects the COVID-19 crisis through the eyes of 12-year-old Dimple Robinson and her family. Dimple's questions convey and explain the nation's challenges and experiences during the tough pandemic.

Since then, many people have asked me, 'What happened to Dimple?'

In *Dimple Dares to Dream,* I return to the Robinson family to find out what they are doing now. Dimple is still the focus, and I show her development from primary to secondary school, where she has made some new friends. Some questions that will be answered include:

Who is Dimple's new best friend? What is her relationship with her brother Adam like? Do they still bicker over who does the washing up? How is Kitty the poodle? Does Nana, the family matriarch, still attend her over-60s club? What is the Windrush generation? Has the pandemic shaped Dimple's character and aspirations, and how does each family member help Dimple fulfil her dream? This book highlights more of her character and strength.

The challenge in writing this book was making the story captivating for the reader while exploring Dimple's character and dream. I hope you find *Dimple Dares to Dream* equally interesting and that you can share in Dimple's dreams and follow your own.

TABLE OF
CONTENTS

>❧<

PROLOGUE

'My baby is graduating! My baby is graduating!' Mum is dancing in front of the large bedroom mirror. She hugs her husband. 'We have done a good job, James.'

'Yes, darling. I still remember when Dimple was born, just like yesterday, and she is now graduating.'

Gloria, Dimple's mum, is an attractive, light-skinned lady in her early forties. She is wearing blue denim jeans and a light blue sweatshirt. Her long, jet-black hair is tied in a braided ponytail. She has added a nude gel nail polish to her short nails. She walks over to her walk-in wardrobe, flicks through her clothes and carefully places a few items on the bed.

'What should I wear, this lemon dress or the blue trouser suit?' she asks Dad, who is sprawled on the bed, reading from his tablet.

'The lemon dress always looks great on you, and the weather will be fine,' he replies absent-mindedly.

'Alright,' Mum says. 'We need to leave early to avoid the morning traffic.'

'Your son is the one who needs to be reminded.'

Mum knocks on her son's bedroom door. 'Adam?'

Adam unsuccessfully tries to switch off the computer game before Mum enters his room. 'Yes, Mum?'

'Have you got everything ready?'

He rises to his feet. Adam is taller than his mum and bears a striking resemblance to his dad. His hair is plaited in neat, backward cornrows. Fixed braces, made of brackets with silver wires, are attached to his teeth.

'You could have knocked before coming into my room, Mum. You always do that!'

'I see your room is untidy as usual, and I don't know how you find anything in this mess.'

'Before you say anything else, Mum, I know we leave at ten.'

'Good. We don't want to be late on your sister's special day. Talking of which, where is Dimple?'

'Princess!' Mum shouts, heading towards Dimple's room. 'Do you need my help with anything?'

A beaming Dimple pokes her head out.

'I'll be fine, Mum. I was just going downstairs to eat.'

'Good idea. You need something in your stomach for your big day ahead. I will come with you and check on Nana.'

Nana's voice travels up the stairs. 'Did someone just call my name?'

'Yes, Nana, how are you getting on with your preparations?' Mum replies, walking downstairs ahead of Dimple.

Nana walks through the pantry carrying a tray of toast and other savoury breakfast items. 'I am fine. Where is that brilliant granddaughter of mine?'

Mum enters the kitchen, boils the kettle, and brings the tea in a teapot, which she then puts on the dining table.

'Good morning, Nana,' Dimple says, hugging her grandmother.

Nana gives Dimple a squeeze. 'I'm so proud of you, darling. Your hard work has paid off. I am going to my granddaughter's graduation! I am as happy as a clam.'

'Thank you, Nana,' Dimple says as she settles on a chair opposite Nana.

Mum starts walking up the carpeted staircase. 'Right, I will leave you two to eat while I finish getting ready. Adam,' she shouts, 'get yourself to the dining table now!'

'Okay, Mum!' Adam saunters past his mother on the stairs, heads towards the dining room and pecks his grandmother on the cheek. 'Morning, Nana. I can't believe my little sister is graduating today.

Adam gives his sister a cute hug, 'I am so proud of you, Dimple.'

'Thanks, Adam. Sit down and eat up, please, so we can leave home on time!'

A new portrait of a three—or four-year-old girl with ringlets resting her head against a fluffy white pillow on her bed is hanging on the dining room wall. A food tray is on her lap, and her small hands are clasped in prayer. She is flanked by a white dog and a brown and white cat.

Nana, Adam, and Dimple tuck into their breakfast.

'I am really proud of both of you,' Nana says.

'I want everyone dressed and by the car in 45 minutes!' Dad shouts from the landing, drying his hair with a small white towel and heading towards his room to get ready.

Soon, everyone is in the car, and Dad reverses onto the main road….

'Dimple! Dimple! Dimple!' Mum repeatedly knocks on her daughter's bedroom door. 'Get up now. You don't want to be late on your first day at your new school.'

Dimple opens her eyes.

Oh no, it was all a dream!

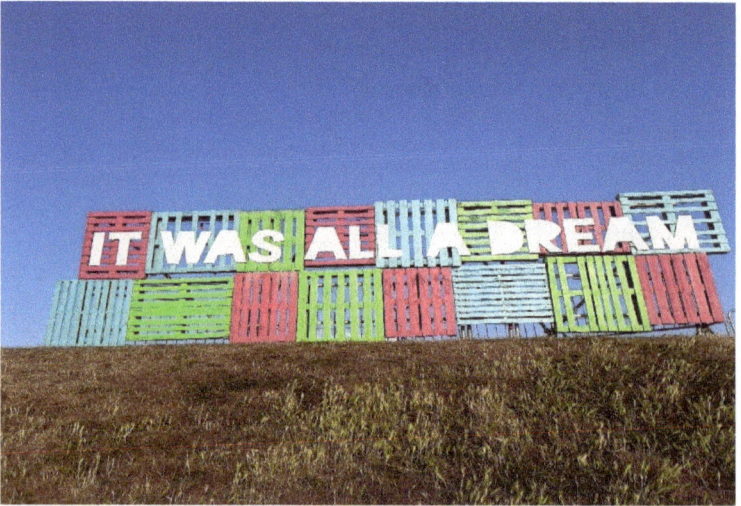

Photo taken by Bola Dada

CHAPTER 1

➤❀❮

Commonwealth Games, Birmingham

The Robinson family are having breakfast on a warm Saturday morning. Given their busy schedules, it is a special occasion whenever the whole family eats together.

Dad sits at the head of the six-seater table with Mum to his right and Adam and Dimple to his left. Adam's breakfast is cereal, Mum and Dimple eat toast and omelette, and Nana sits opposite Dad with her usual bowl of porridge and blueberries.

'Dad, I have applied to attend Birmingham University's Open Day next month,' Adam says.

'That's interesting, Son,' Dad replies between mouthfuls of toast and omelette.

'I thought you were going to military school,' Dimple chips in. She is taken aback by her brother's announcement.

'When did you start thinking of going to University?' Nana asks.

'I think we should all go easy on him,' Mum says. 'We respect your decision, Adam. Let us know when you want to discuss this some more.'

'There's really nothing to discuss,' Adam replies. 'It's just an Open Day to talk to current students and staff and see what the campus looks like.'

'What are you looking to study?' Dad asks.

'Psychology.'

'That's around the same time as the Birmingham games,' Nana remarks, changing the subject.

'I will try and get some leave for that time,' Mum says. 'We can kill two birds with one stone - attend the Open Day and participate in the Commonwealth Games.'

'I dare say tickets to the Games will be long gone by this time,' Dad points out.

'We can still experience the Games ambience,' Dimple says. 'Are all the Commonwealth countries taking part?'

'Someone please pass me the honey,' Nana says.

Mum gets up to give Nana the jar of honey. 'Between fifty-six and seventy-four countries take part in the Commonwealth Games. It's up to each country to decide whether to participate.'

Dimple peeps over Nana's shoulders, more interested in what her grandmother is searching for than what Mum has to say. 'What are you doing, Nana?' She asks with a cheeky smile.

'Using Google to learn more about the Games,' Nana says proudly. The motto for this year's event is 'Games for Everyone.'

'You are breaking your own rules, Nana!' Dimple exclaims, imitating Nana's voice. 'How often have I told you not to bring your phone to the dining table?'

'Nana Microsoft!' Adam says playfully while Dimple starts clapping and singing:

'Go Nana!

Go Nana!

Go Nana!

My Nana is the best, and that I know.

'Cos she can use Google like no one else.

C'mon Google, tell Nana Microsoft all about the
Birmingham Commonwealth Games!

Nana, Mum, and Dad erupt into fits of laughter.

'I will look into available hotels in Birmingham,' Dad says after they've calmed down.

'I believe the university has a hotel,' Adam says.

'How many hours will it take to drive to Birmingham?' Dimple asks.

'About three hours from London.' Mum replies. 'Does that sound right, James?'

'It should be about that length of time, but you can never predict the situation on the M40 motorway,' Dad says.

'I have something to look forward to, then,' Dimple says excitedly, dancing up and down the kitchen diner. 'I can't wait to tell all my friends!'

'Nana, what do you have planned for today?' Mum asks.

'John and I are going to the park around 11. I offered to walk Kitty and give her some exercise since Dimple has not been out with her recently. The park will be less busy since the park-run event will be over by then.

'I have been busy with my schoolwork,' Dimple says. 'Thank you for helping Kitty exercise today, Nana.'

'Anytime, pet. It allows John and me to catch up with news from the over-60s Club.

'I will leave home before you, Nana.' Adam says. 'Ollie and Jay are accompanying me to the park run event.'

✿ ✿ ✿ ✿ ✿ ✿ ✿ ✿

A few days later, it's time to travel to Birmingham, and the family is preparing for the three-hour journey.

Dad is wearing a black T-shirt over khaki shorts and black trainers. His glasses are tinted from the sun's rays. He gives the Camper van a final check and then enters the postcode into the Satnav.

Dimple walks out of the house with Kitty in her arms. She bears a striking resemblance to her mum, with brown eyes, an oval face, and a slightly higher neck. She also sports a few pimples on her forehead and a dimple on her left cheek that becomes prominent when she smiles. Today, she is wearing a pink T-shirt over a pair of blue jeans, and her hair is parted in two, each part tied with blue ribbons. Her pink sandals match her top.

Kitty, the white poodle Nana gave Dimple on her 12th birthday, wears a silver chain around her neck with a pendant bearing the letter 'K'.

'Please help with the rest of the luggage, Dimple.' Adam grumbles, dragging the suitcases to the van. He is in a black tracksuit with white stripes.

Nana's yellow summer dress has white petal buttons scattered across the front, with a yellow sunhat and yellow ribbon, completed with tan sandals. She also has a pair of sunglasses on and drapes a brown bag over her shoulders.

Mum checks that the blinds are drawn, and all electrical appliances are switched off. She removes the milk bottle from the fridge and empties it into the kitchen sink. In a blue jeans jumpsuit and black medium-heeled wedges, her long braids reach down to her waist.

As she eventually exits the house towards the van, the summery scent of her perfume engulfs the air.

'That's a nice perfume you have on, Gloria,' Nana remarks.

'Thanks, Nana. The children gave it to me on Mother's Day.' Mum turns to Dad. 'James, have you given Franklin a spare set of the house keys? He may need access to the house in an emergency.'

Dad searches his pockets. 'Not yet, dear. I will do so now.' He heads next door and presses the bell.

Franklin appears almost immediately from where he has been spying on his neighbours through his window blinds.

'Hi, James. All set to travel?' he asks with a smile.

'Yes, we're ready.' James hands over the spare keys. 'Thank you once again.'

'Happy to be of service as usual. You do the same for me. Enjoy your trip.'

Dad returns to the van and takes his position behind the steering wheel. Mum is in the front passenger seat, and Adam and Dimple occupy the middle seats, leaving Nana to sit at the back.

Dad turns on the radio and reverses carefully onto the main road, checking his mirrors on both sides.

'Are we staying at the Edgbaston Park Hotel and Conference Centre?' Dimple asks as they drive through the town.

'We were not able to book that,' Mum replies. 'We were fortunate to snap up an Air BnB in the town centre. Every hotel and accommodation is fully booked.'

As the car moves sleekly through the motorway, Dad drives past Windsor and Milton Keynes, and the family take in the signage to other cities.

'I'm surprised the traffic is not queuing on our side of the road,' Nana says.

'But the opposite side is busy,' Mum points out. 'Car after car seems stuck in a queue that isn't moving.'

The Birmingham Games' news filters in through the radio. Tourists from all over the world are already arriving in the city, and the Prince of Wales (Prince Charles), accompanied by The Duchess of Cornwall, will represent Her Majesty the Queen and officially open the Games in front of over 30,000 spectators at the newly refurbished Alexander Stadium and an estimated global television audience of over one billion people.

There is a traffic queue as Dad exits the motorway and drives into Birmingham town. 'There are lots of road works,' Dimple says, looking ahead. 'That's why the cars are not moving.'

Dad drives up a bridge.

'The shops are the same as those in London,' Adam remarks. 'There is a Subway shop to our left and Greggs to the right.'

Nana shifts in her seat and stretches her neck. 'I am already tired. I didn't think the journey would knock me out.'

'I'm hungry,' Dimple moans.

'James, why don't we drive to a restaurant before going to our apartment?' Mum says.

'Good idea. Everyone, look out for restaurants along the way,' Dad announces. 'I need to fill up on petrol first, though.'

'There is a filling station ahead on the other side of the road,' Mum points out.

Dad navigates to the mini roundabout, turns right, and drives for a few minutes till they reach the filling station. He fills up the tank, picks up some chewing gum from the counter and pays for the petrol and gum. Back at the car, he passes the chewing gum to Mum, who passes it on to Adam and Dimple. They drive away from the filling station.

'Look, there's a Harvester!' Nana exclaims.

Dad pulls up outside the restaurant. Mum gets out and slides open the door for the rest of the family.

'Oh, my poor legs!' Nana looks around the car park before heading inside.

'Table for how many, please?' asks a young, clean-shaven, cheerful waiter in a white shirt with rolled-up sleeves. He is holding a small tablet in his hands.

'Five,' Dad says.

'And my poodle makes six of us, thank you!' Dimple adds.

Mum leans towards Nana. 'When Dimple smiles and flashes her dimple, she is trying to make a statement,' she says quietly. 'She must be trying to charm the waiter into letting Kitty into the restaurant.'

'I'm sorry, we do not allow dogs inside,' the lad says, 'but you can choose a table outside.'

'We'll do that, then,' Dad announces.

They walk out of the restaurant, and the waiter leads them to a table under a big parasol. 'Take your seats, please, while I get you the menu,' he says.

When he returns, Dimple orders pasta from the kid's menu. Adam wants six wings and a burger with chips (and burger sauce), while Nana orders a salmon dish, and Mum and

Dad ask for some chicken with home-baked jacket potatoes, peas, ratatouille, and the speciality chicken gravy.

'Dimple, eat your food slowly!' Nana remarks. 'You will cover your beautiful top in pasta sauce at this rate.'

Dimple is munching as fast as possible. 'Nana, I am hungry after that long drive!'

Just then, Adam opens his mouth wide to engulf his burger.

'Nana, you should be talking to Adam,' Dimple snorts. 'I can see his molars from here!'

Everyone laughs.

Nana looks around the table, grateful to share this time with her family.

'Dad, remember our last holiday during lockdown?' Dimple says, feeding scraps of food to Kitty, who smiles contentedly. 'You stopped at the Motorway service area, and I went into McDonalds to get a milkshake…'

'Yes, and you didn't get your favourite flavour.'

Dimple rolls her eyes. 'No, Dad, there were no milkshakes at all!'

'KFC also ran out of chicken supplies around the same time,' Nana adds.

'How did we survive?' Adam asks, sounding amazed.

They finish eating, and Mum pays with her card.

'Does anyone want to use the restroom before we continue to the Air B&B?' Dad asks.

Mum, Nana, and Dimple head off to the Ladies. Adam looks for the Gents, and Dad takes Kitty to the car. When they return, Dad enters the destination address into the Satnav, showing they are 15 minutes away.

He puts the music radio on, and they soon return to the apartment.

❋ ❋ ❋ ❋ ❋ ❋ ❋ ❋

'You have reached your destination…' the Satnav repeatedly announces. Before long, Dad is trying to figure out which apartment they booked.

'Alright! Alright, Satnav! We hear you,' He blurts out, turning off the car engine.

Adam steps out with Dimple behind him.

'Let's see who will guess the correct apartment,' Dimple says.

Adam points to the left. 'I say it's this building.'

'And I choose the one opposite us,' Dimple quips.

Dad checks his phone, looks left and right, checks his phone again and points to the building in front.

'Yes!' Dimple dances around, making faces at her brother. 'I won!'

Mum gets the keys, and they head to the front door of the two-storey house.

'It appears to be divided into six flats – two flats over three floors,' Nana says as they enter the building.

Dimple reads out the door numbers. 'We are looking for Number 25, and since 23 and 24 are on the ground floor, our flat must be on the middle floor.

Two flights of stairs later, number 25 is there on the right. Mum hands Dad the keys, he opens the door, and they explore the flat. First, Mum and Nana check their faces and pat their hair at the large gold-plated mirror opposite the front door.

Adam slides past them and opens the door to a fair-sized living room containing a large-screen television and a black dining table with four matching black chairs. The grey six-sitter curved settee fits perfectly into the room, along with a grey foot-stand. Beside a small black table and blue office chair that can be used as a workspace, a door leads to a small balcony.

Dimple points downstairs. 'I can see our car!'

Dad comes up behind her. 'I hope it is safe to park on the street like that.'

'I like the ambience.' Mum says. 'The neighbourhood is quiet and peaceful.'

'Look at the boats under the bridge,' Dimple points towards the low bridge. 'There is a canal!'

'It looks like a nice area, love,' Nana says.

Mum nods. 'Let's see what the rest of the flat looks like.'

They walk into a moderate-sized newly built kitchen decorated in grey. The American-style fridge freezer, microwave, cooker, and toaster are grey, but the air-fryer is black.

Next, Dad leads the way to the main bedroom on the right beside a storage space and drops his light travel bag on the floor.

Adam snaps the smallest room with the blue décor and throws his jacket on the bed.

'I guess that leaves me with the room with the brown wallpaper; it is a good-sized room, though,' Nana says as she puts her luggage by the built-in wardrobe.

Dimple inspects the restrooms. 'I like it when a flat has a separate bathroom and toilet.'

'Thank God the apartment is neat,' Adam says. 'I always dread how an Air B&B will turn out.'

'I will share Nana's room,' Dimple announces.

Mum looks doubtful. 'You will most likely end up sleeping in Adam's room because he will probably sleep on the settee watching films or playing his games.'

'You're right about that, Mum,' Adam replies.

'I'll make us all something to drink.' Nana says, heading for the living room.

Dimple drops her bags in Nana's room and follows her to the kitchen, lightly stroking Kitty's head in her arms. *She tells herself that Kitty's doughnut-shaped bed can stay in the space between the kitchen and Adam's room.*

'Where will Kitty sleep tonight?' Nana asks as Dimple enters the kitchen.

'I was thinking of the little space along the corridor.'

Nana opens the fridge to see what is inside. 'Or she could sleep by the television in the living room.'

'That's a better idea! Thanks, Nana. I will place her sleeping bag by the TV.

The family settle down in the living room with their drinks.

'I'm going to have a nice, hot shower first,' Mum says, picking up her drink and taking it to the bedroom.

Nana nods. 'Good idea. I will have my shower just before bed.'

Dad turns on the television.

'No football channel, please, Dad!' Dimple begs.

'There are no football channels here, anyway,' Dad says.

They watch a drama, and as soon as the programme finishes, Dad lurches to his feet. 'Right, everyone! Get ready to leave the house by nine tomorrow morning. We will have breakfast on our way to the University.'

Dimple thinks he looks a little tired, *probably from all that driving earlier.*

Mum gets to her feet, too. 'James, we can do some food shopping after the tour, so we don't have to spend a fortune eating out.'

I don't feel that sleepy, but a nine am start needs an early bedtime. Dimple decides. 'Speaking of eating…I am going to bake a cake with the air fryer for tea one evening before we go back home.'

'Have you practised baking with the air fryer before, love?' Dad asks.

'Yes, Dad. It's quite easy, and the cake turns out nice. I watched a lady describing the process on TV. Then I practised with Nana while you were at work.'

�֎ �֎ �֎ �֎ ✖ ✖ ✖ ✖ ✖

Everyone is in the car by 9 a.m. the following day. They stop at a café for breakfast and soon head to Birmingham University.

Adam is keen to see what the city looks like. Lots of people are milling about. Some are walking while others commute by public transport or in their cars.

'Seeing so many people moving about makes me wonder how far we are from the Games venue,' Dimple says.

Adam is rolling his eyes. 'There's more than one venue, Dimple.'

'The university is straight ahead.' Nana points out.

'I can see the signs!' Dimple says excitedly.

Dad drives slowly into the campus, parks the car, and everyone alights from the vehicle.

Mum slips her sunglasses on. 'What a beautiful place.'

'I agree,' Dad says. 'It is green and spacious.'

There are check-in booths across the campus. A student approaches and hands Dad a map to help them navigate. Dad thanks her politely, and they move towards the library.

Staff and student ambassadors are based at the campus' key entry points, wearing bright green "Ask Me" T-shirts. They are hard to miss. The student ambassadors point guests in the right direction if they want to see any places of interest and help plan the day.

'Is there anywhere you want to visit today particularly?' the student ambassador asks. She looks about 19 years old, with a nerdy face and black hair tinted with blue fringes.

'Do you know where the psychology department is?' Adam asks.

'That would be in the Faculty of Social Sciences.' She opens a map. 'Let me show you.'

'Thank you, young lady,' Mum says.

'What is your name, dear?' Nana asks.

'Geraldine, but everyone calls me Geri.'

'Will the nursing department be in the same building, Geri?' Dimple chimes in.

'Are you coming to the university, too?' Geri teases Dimple.

'I'm keeping my options open, but I want to be a nurse like my mum and Grandma.'

'Oh, that's lovely,' Geri says.

Adam thanks her, and they walk towards the faculty, where Adam asks one of the lecturers questions about the course. They visit the student accommodation to check out the available facilities. Prospective students move like a sea of heads in different directions along the corridors and courtyards, all looking intrigued.

'It's nearly time for our event at the Commonwealth Games,' Nana finally says.

'Luckily, Dad's colleague passed on his family tickets to us,' Adam says.

'Yes, shame that they could not attend the games,' Dad replies. 'We should make our way.'

'Adam, are you happy with what you've seen today?' Mum asks.

'Yes, I think I'm okay, thanks,' Adam says. 'The accommodation is neat and close to the faculties.'

'I hope you get into this university,' Dimple says. 'I love the atmosphere.'

Soon, they arrive at the Alexander Stadium to watch the Women's 100m hurdles.

'How do we find our seats among all these people in the grandstand?' Dimple scans the stadium with her eyes,

'I hope we get the rail seats to have a good view,' Adam says.

They shuffle among the other spectators. 'Looks like we are sitting in Row J, seats 40 to 44,' Mum says, reading the seat numbers from the tickets she is holding.

Nana carefully holds on to the rail and steps up to her allocated seat. She pushes the seat down. 'These seats are rugged and vandal-proof.'

'They are steel rail seats,' Mum says, sitting beside Nana.

'I hope they are comfortable too,' Dad says.

Adam points towards the billboard. 'The University of Birmingham is one of the sponsors. How cool!'

Mum puts on her sunglasses and takes pictures of the stadium with her phone. 'The blue tracks in the middle of the red ground are absolutely beautiful.'

The lady behind taps Mum on the shoulder. 'Would you mind sitting down? You are blocking my view.'

'Oh, I apologise,' Mum says as she takes her seat.

Despite sitting beside each other, Adam and Dimple exchange a 'surprised' emoji on their phones at the lady's remark.

'The participants are already in place,' Nana points out. 'Ready, and off they go!'

The whistle goes.

'Oh, they are ever so fast!' Dimple screams.

'Look at that!' Dad yells. 'Did you all see that? Tobi Amusan won with a 12.30.'

The whole family jump up to clap and cheer for Tobi Amusan.

Nana claps loudly. 'Her family must be very proud of her.'

'Most Africans prefer their children to be doctors, lawyers, engineers, and so on. Tobi is proof that the African mentality of sports not being a serious career is false,' Mum says.

'Shouldn't you follow your dream?' Dimple asks.

Nana pats Dimple on the shoulder. 'Yes, following your heart and your dream is important.'

'She may need to think of what to do when she is too old to compete,' Dad remarks. 'That is where a good education comes in. She could start a business or coach the younger athletes.'

'I think that is probably a long time away,' Mum says.

'Hats off to her,' Nana says, 'With her 12.30-second win, she broke the 16-year record and defended her Gold Coast 2018 Commonwealth Games title while she was at it.'

'She should enjoy this moment,' Adam says.

Prince Edward, The Earl of Wessex and Vice-Patron of the Commonwealth Games Federation, officially closes the Games with the words: 'You have inspired us and hopefully future generations. You have also demonstrated what unites us.'

CHAPTER 2

>❀<

My Mum, My Hero

'Mum, I can't find my phone charger, and my battery is almost dead!'

'You are old enough to look after your things, Dimple. Don't forget to pack your hair attachments and take your hair cream.'

Wearing a black T-shirt, joggers with white stripes, and trainers, Dimple flips through her duvet cover and then searches under her bed. Kitty wags her tail against Dimple's legs. Dimple strokes her ears, and they start rummaging around the room.

Kitty thinks it's a game.

'Hurry up!' Mum says. 'We don't want to miss your appointment with Jade.' Jade, Mum's hairdresser for more than five years, also looks after Nana's hair.

The rest of the family is out. Dimple and Mum leave the house, and as she moves the car out of the driveway, Mum tells Dimple to message the family WhatsApp Group that they are off to the hair salon.

Dimple puts her headphones on and sends the text.

'Do you know what style you are having today?' Mum asks.

Dimple doesn't reply.

Mum snaps her fingers to grab Dimple's attention and repeats her question.

'Oh, I don't know. Jade usually shows me some styles, and I pick what I like.' She puts her headphones back on.

Mum parks on a side street, and they walk a short distance to the salon.

Jade greets them as they enter. 'Hello Gloria, Dimple!'

'How have you been, Jade?' Mum asks.

Jade pats her stomach. 'Very well.'

Mum smiles affectionately. 'Oh! I see you have a little bun in the oven.'

Jade pats her bump again. 'Yes, this little one is due next month.'

'You should take things slowly,' Mum says. 'You shouldn't be on your feet for long periods.'

'I know,' Jade replies, 'but I'm working for as long as possible to have more time with this little one when he or she arrives.'

'Are you having a boy or a girl?' Dimple asks.

'No, we decided against finding out the gender. My husband and I want it to be a surprise. Come over here, Dimple. Let's get you ready to go back to school. Here,' She shows Dimple some photographs on her phone. 'Which style do you want?'

Dimple points at the black braids with the grey strips in the front.

'That's the 'Kem' style,' Jade says.

'Why Kem?' Mum asks.

Jade laughs. 'It is a favourite of Kemi Badenoch, the Conservative MP. It is more popular because she is a favourite to be the next Tory leader.'

'Oh, I see!' Mum laughs.

'Are you looking forward to going back to school, Dimple?' Jade asks.

Nodding, Dimple returns the phone to Jade.

'She has settled down well in her new school,' Mum interjects. 'She also travels home on the school bus with her friends.'

Jade drapes a black protective gown around Dimple and seals the back with tape.

'Gloria, do you mind if Adele washes Dimple's hair while I have my lunch? I am so hungry, and I wonder why.' She laughs.

'Not at all, but I would like you to braid her hair yourself.'

Jade asks her staff, Adele, to wash Dimple's hair before retrieving her lunch box from the inner office. She re-enters the salon, finds a quiet corner and starts eating.

Adele leads Dimple to a basin in the back corner, shampoos her hair twice and adds conditioner. She then sits for 30 minutes before Adele rinses off the conditioner and leads Dimple back to the front of the salon. She swaps the wet towel for a dry one and blow-dries Dimple's hair.

Jade walks over with one hand on her hip and the other cradling her big stomach. Dimple can see her through the large mirror opposite. She puts her headphones on to listen to some music while Mum continues chatting with Jade.

'So, is this baby number three?'

Jade smiles. 'Number two. My boy is two years old. Secretly, I would love this one to be a girl, but all I pray for is a healthy child. As a child, I always dreamt of having a little girl I can pamper and do girly things with.'

'Yeah, it is lovely to have a girl. She will be lucky indeed to have you as her mum because her hair will be well taken care of.'

'Dimple, do you want the parting in the middle or to the side?'

'She cannot hear anyone with that thing over her ears,' Mum says.

Jade smiles and bends down to speak into Dimple's ear, but as she bends over, her knees go all wobbly, and she falls. Dimple is oblivious, but Mum realises what has happened and rushes over to Jade.

'Oh my God!' Adele shrieks.

Dimple looks up, removes her headphones, and squats on the floor beside Jade.

Now in 'work' mode, Mum folds her sweatshirt's sleeves inward and removes Jade's apron.

'Get me some towels, Adele,' she says calmly.

A frightened Adele hurries off and returns with a few towels.

'Dimple, place a rolled-up towel under Jade's right hip while I tilt her slightly to the left,' Mum instructs. 'This will facilitate blood flow for Mum and baby.'

Mum does the DR **ABC** check – an acronym for the steps to take when dealing with a collapsed person. DR ABC stands for:

- Danger
- Response
- Airway
- Breathing
- Circulation / CPR

She shakes Jade gently. 'Are you okay, Jade?'

There is no response.

Gloria places one hand on the other in the centre of Jade's chest and begins light chest compressions. Dimple calls an ambulance from her phone. She gets the address from Adele and passes on the information to the call-handling agent.

'Is anyone else there with you?' the agent asks.

'My mum is helping her,' Dimple says. 'She is a nurse.'

'That is incredibly good,' the man on the other end says. 'My name is Cecil. Put your phone on the speaker while I speak to your mum.'

Dimple complies.

'Hi. My name is Gloria, and I am a theatre nurse.'

'Do you know what happened?' Cecil asks.

'My hairdresser is pregnant, and she is due next month. She collapsed while styling my daughter's hair. I believe it is a maternal Cardiac Arrest from sheer exhaustion.'

'OK, please keep her stable. An ambulance is already on its way.'

'Don't worry, Adele, Mum will look after Jade,' Dimple says.

As she consoles Adele, Dimple hears the approaching sirens. 'It's the ambulance!' she exclaims and hurries outside. A small crowd outside and peep through the salon's transparent window.

Two paramedics shove them aside before hurrying into the salon. They are dressed in green short-sleeved shirts over black trousers with large side pockets.

'Where is the patient?' one of them asks.

'Over here, please!' Mum waves and the paramedics move over to where she is kneeling. 'Her name is Jade.'

The taller man kneels next to Mum. 'Jade, can you hear me? My name is Christian, and this is my assistant, Andre.'

They gently lift Jade onto a stretcher on the floor, and then Christian puts an oxygen mask over her mouth.

'Call Jade's husband and tell him what happened,' Mum tells Adele.

The paramedics finish their checks before carrying Jade to the ambulance. The crowd make way, but they hover around, watching the ambulance drive off.

'Do you think Jade and the baby will be okay, Mum?'

'Yes, darling. The doctors will put her on bed rest till her baby arrives.'

'I'm proud of you, Mum,' Dimple says.

'I don't know what I would have done without you, Mrs Robinson,' says Adele, who now has the task of finishing Dimple's braids.

Mum phones Nana and tells her what happened.

'Poor thing! Will she be okay?'

'She'll be fine. She has been working too hard and needs to take things easy until the baby is born.'

'When I grow up, I want to look after people and save lives,' Dimple announces.

➤❀⬿

CHAPTER 3

The Beginning of Term

It is a bright Tuesday morning, and the air is fresh. The summer holiday is over, and Dimple is excited to begin the new school year. She finished Year 8 with excellent grades and starts in Year 9 today. She is no longer the new kid at school.

She tried catching up with her friends—Zainab, Natalie, Amara, Sophia, and Favour—during the school holidays by text and Snapchat. Zainab and Natalie still attend the same school, while Dimple attends a school with Sophia.

'Zainab is now in my Maths group,' Natalie tells her friends on their Snapchat.

Zainab texts back immediately. 'Yes, Mum booked extra classes for me over the school holidays. Our Maths teacher noticed the improvement and moved me up.'

Yesterday was an Inset Day at Dimple's school, with only the teachers attending to prepare for the students' return to school. So today is the first day Dimple will see Sophia after the holidays.

Nana is making Dimple's lunch in the kitchen.

'Good morning, Nana!' There is a spring in Dimple's step as she reaches the dining table in her crisp, new school uniform – a white V-neck blouse, a black skirt, black tights and shoes, and a maroon jumper. She will put on her school hat after breakfast.

Nana hands her the lunch box. 'Morning, pet. Are you ready for your first day back at school?'

Dimple sits at the table. 'Yes, Nana. Did you make my packed lunch?' She opens the box to see what is inside.

'Yes, It's a tuna sandwich. I thought you'd like your favourite lunch on your first day back.'

The dimple on Dimple's left cheek flashes as she hugs her grandmother. 'Thanks, Nana – You're the best!'

Dressed in a green maxi made from African prints, matching large green earrings and a white turban, Nana sits opposite Dimple with a bowl of porridge, blueberries, and strawberries.

'We can't have you going hungry, especially since you don't enjoy the school dinners. You never know, however. They may have new cooks or new recipes this year.'

Dimple bites into her toast and marmalade, picks up her phone and starts typing a message.

'Dimple Robinson!' Nana scolds. 'How often have I told you not to bring your phone to the dining table?'

'Sorry, Nana, I'm texting Sophia about where to meet at school. I can't wait to see my friends today after the long summer holiday.'

'That's understandable. But be quick about it,' Nana replies.

Dimple puts the phone down to drink her hot cocoa. 'Thank you, Nana.'

'I don't understand how you can drink cocoa in the morning,' Nana says. 'Hot cocoa makes me feel sleepy. Why don't you try having tea before you go to school and hot cocoa before bed?'

Dimple rolls her eyes. 'I don't like the taste of tea. It's hot cocoa or hot chocolate for me any time of the day.'

Mum descends gracefully from the stairs in a blue T-shirt over black leggings and loafers. Her hair is tied back with a blue band, and her only makeup is lip gloss, but she still looks pretty.

'If you don't go to the car now, you will be late, Dimple!'

'I'm ready, Mum,' Dimple replies. 'I'll just pop upstairs for my school bag. Is Dad ready for work?'

'Your dad is working from home today, Miss. Hurry up, or we will be stuck in traffic. I won't make any excuses to your teachers if you are late to school.'

Dimple dashes up the stairs, two steps at a time.

Dad appears from his room and shakes his head. 'Princess, I have told you time and time again; don't run up the stairs, or you will hurt yourself one of these days.'

Dimple grabs her bag and gives her dad a peck on the cheek. 'I'm all right, Dad. Mum is dropping me off at school. See you in the evening. I love you!'

'Love you too, darling. Have a good day at school.'

'Bye Nana!' Dimple waves and dashes out to meet Mum.

'You're forgetting something, Miss,' Nana yells.

'My lunch!' Dimple runs back inside the house to grab her lunch box. 'Thanks again, Nana.'

Mum is already behind the steering wheel of her red Ford KA. Dimple comes out of the house and joins her. As Mum reverses out of the drive, Dimple waves at Franklin, who is setting out for his morning walk with Terry, his corgi.

'Morning, Gloria! Is Dimple back at school?'

'Yes, Franklin,' Dimple replies before Mum can say anything. 'I will be choosing my subjects this year.'

'She is not sure if she wants to do science subjects or Arts,' Mum adds.

'I'm sure there is plenty of time to do that.' Franklin says with a grin. 'Well, look after yourself, young lady, and have a good day, both of you.'

As they travel along, the traffic is relatively quiet. They should make the 45-minute journey in no time.

Dimple observes the people around her. Students of all ages in different school uniforms are at the bus stop beside their house. They are all smartly dressed and chatting animatedly, oblivious to the time and other people around them. Hearing their laughter as Mum drives past increases Dimple's desire to see her friends as soon as possible.

'So, have you considered what subjects you will choose this year?'

'I'm not sure yet.'

'What do you want to do when you grow up? What are your dreams, and who inspires you? These will all help you make the right decision.'

'I like helping people, and I love animals,' Dimple says.

'Then you could consider being a Veterinary doctor, a social worker, or a teacher. There are loads of careers to choose from. Just look around you.'

'Will do. Thank you, Mum.'

'Did you pack everything you need for school today, darling?' Mum asks.

'Yes, Mum. I packed my bag yesterday, and Nana made my lunch this morning.'

'That's kind of Nana.' Mum pulls into a spot outside the school gates. 'Remember to join the school bus on time for your journey home later.'

'I'll be on the bus with Sophia as usual,' Dimple replies. She kisses her mum on the cheek and gets out of the car. 'Thanks for the ride, Mum! See you later.' She walks inside the school gates.

A giant sign depicting the school's name and logo is the first noticeable thing. The building is old-style, but a bit of greenery in the middle gives it a fresh look. There are two entrance doors made of glass. The left door leads to the boy's school and the right to the girl's school. The reception area in the middle of the hall connects the schools.

Sophia walks in. 'Hey, Dimple!' The friends hug each other warmly.

'How have you been?' Dimple asks.

'Very well. I like your keyring, Dimple.'

'I bought it when we went to Scotland last year. It was lovely to get away, and for Nana to see her old friends. The journey was long, but we had comfort breaks.'

'Is Scotland as cold as people say?'

''It can be, but we had pleasant weather because we went in the summer.'

'The pictures I have seen are mostly of old, grey buildings, not attractive.'

'There are some modern houses too,' Dimple says. 'Did you know that Harry Potter was written in Edinburgh?'

Sophia shakes her head. 'Nope.'

'Mum, Nana, and I visited a café called *The Elephant House*, where J.K. Rowling wrote her later novels. It is the best-known Harry Potter location in Edinburgh. We even had snacks there, and we took lots of pictures!'

'You are lucky to have relatives outside London. My family are based here, which is quite boring. We did not go anywhere for the holidays, but I joined a summer club, where we did some creative writing and poetry and had dance lessons,' Sophia says.

'Oh, that is lovely! I quite like poetry, too.' Dimple replies.

'Guess what?' Dimple says.

Sophia opens her eyes wide. 'What?'

'We recently went to Birmingham to see If Adam would like to go to University there.'

'Really? You never mentioned that!' Sophia rolls her eyes in amazement at her friend.

'It was a last-minute sort of thing, and we got to see an event at the Birmingham Commonwealth games,' Dimple says, opening her hand casually.

'You never! Dimple Robinson, you lucky girl!'

'Well, it just kind of happened that Dad got some tickets from his colleague, and we had already made plans to go and check out the University.'

'How come you are always so lucky?'

'You get to do some nice things too.'

'Not half as nice as you. I like how you do things as a family.'

Dimple shrugs.

The assembly bell rings and the girls move to the school hall. The big, impressive room comfortably accommodates up to five hundred children. Two black curtains on either side of the stage are drawn apart, and a student plays the organ. The children are seated in rows, with the older ones at the back of the hall and the younger students in front. The teachers sit in front to the right, but each Head of Year sits with the students in the centre. The others excitedly catch up on their holiday gossip. Then, everyone rises as the prefects from Year 12 and Year 13 walk in.

The Head girl reads a poem titled '*New Beginnings*.'

'*New Beginnings*' describes the first day of secondary school, when the incoming students' parents are more nervous than their wards. It talks about making new friends and embracing new opportunities.

The headteacher, Mr Cipolla, walks up to the stage, and the noise gradually fades. He taps the microphone to check if it is working.

'Alright, alright, that's enough!' he says. 'I know you are excited to see each other. I hope you rested well and are ready for the new school year. The new Year 7 students joined us last week. Hopefully, you will help them find their feet. Remember how you felt when you did not know anyone on your first day

> **"**
> *The more you read, the more things you will know. The more you learn, the more places you'll go*
> *– Dr Seuss.*
> **"**

in Year 7? Who helped you find your way around, and what did they do to make you feel you belonged?

'We have some new teachers too. Miss Isabella Brown joins us as the Year 9 English teacher, while Mr Philip Isaiah is Year 11's additional science teacher. Let us work hard together and have a fun, great, and exciting school year.'

There is a round of applause from the students, and the teachers get up to leave. After the staff, the Heads of Year and the students stand up and file out of the hall, starting with the back row.

CHAPTER 4

>✤<

Dimple Makes Friends
with Iryna

It is lunchtime. The basement school canteen is in an open plan area with grey and white décor. A middle glass door leads to a short flight of stairs to the main reception area. The other door leads along a corridor to the sports and post rooms. In the main serving area, canteen staff in white cotton caps and aprons stand behind the counter, ready to serve the hungry students, while the kitchen is behind the staff. A few posters on the wall include the week's menu and notices that read, *'Remember to eat your five portions of fruits and vegetables a day'* and *'Be respectful to canteen staff'*.

The aroma of the hot food is enticing, and the students immediately join the queue, waiting patiently while chatting in little groups and looking around for any familiar faces they missed from the morning assembly.

Dimple is eating her packed lunch. Tamara, who is of mixed heritage (her mum is from Nigeria, and her dad is English), joins Dimple, carrying a plate of macaroni cheese, followed by Sophia and Jane, also from her year group.

'Your food looks nice,' Dimple says to Tamara. 'I love macaroni cheese!'

'The new chef has changed the menus, and the food is tasty,' Sophia says as she settles down to eat her fries and fish fillet.

'Plus, the food is served hot,' Jane says. 'I think the new food containers keep them hot for longer.'

'I might try the canteen food then,' Dimple says. 'It will save Nana getting up early to prepare my lunch.'

'I wish they had more Chinese food like sweet and sour pork,' Sophia, who is half-Romanian and half-Chinese, says between mouthfuls.

With Jane and Tamara backing the serving area, Dimple and Sophia, sitting opposite, have an unobstructed view of the students entering the canteen.

'Sophia, what do you think of the new girl who joined our class last week?' Dimple asks.

'I don't like her,' Sophia says, 'She keeps to herself all the time. Maybe she thinks she's better than the rest of us.'

'Don't be too quick to judge her,' Dimple replies. 'Remember when we were fresh students too?'

'Has anyone tried to involve her in activities so she does not feel like an outsider?' Tamara asks. The oldest of the four, Tamara's hair is in two plaits with a maroon ribbon at the end of each tail. 'For all we know, she could just be shy.'

'Hush!' Jane exclaims suddenly. 'Don't look back now, but the new girl just joined the queue.

'I see her,' Dimple says, casting a sneaky look. 'I like her shoes, and she's very neat. I just wish she were more friendly.'

'What do you know about this new girl?' Jane asks.

'Not much,' Dimple says.

'We know she's from another country,' Sophia adds.

'So, you can understand why she keeps to herself,' Jane says.

'When I was about five years old, our neighbours would not let their children play with me at first,' Tamara says. 'It took Mum being nice to them when we met on the streets and in the park before they finally accepted me.'

'That must have been hard for you,' Jane says.

'It was. I kept asking my parents if we could move to another area, but things settled down eventually, and I made some nice friends.'

'What is everyone doing this weekend?' Dimple asks. 'We are going to my cousin's house tomorrow. It's Samuel's birthday, and the whole family is going to celebrate with him.'

'Is he off to Uni this year then?' Sophia asks.

'No, next year. His older brother David starts this year.'

'What present are you giving to Samuel?' Jane asks.

'I'm going to bake him some cupcakes, but I'm struggling to think of the right present for him.'

'Get him a football shirt, boots, a mug or anything football-related, and he'll be fine,' Sophia says.

They fall about giggling. *Boys and football*!

'I will get Mum to buy the present,' Dimple says.

The new girl sits by herself at the table beside them. Next thing, Dimple goes to sit opposite her.

'What does Dimple think she's doing?' Tamara whispers to the others.

'I really have no clue,' Jane says.

Sophia's eyes are wide with disbelief. 'Me neither.'

'Hello, my name is Dimple. I am in Year 9,' Dimple says with a warm smile.

The new girl does not know how to react or what to say.

'What is your name?'

'I... I... My name is… is Iryna,' the girl finally replies.

'You have such lovely eyes and hair,' Dimple says.

Tha Thannnk you,' Iryna says shyly, putting some food in her mouth and hoping Dimple will stop asking questions.

But Dimple continues. 'Do you live close to the school?'

Chewing slowly, Iryna nods without maintaining eye contact.

'Do you like the school?' Dimple asks again.

Iryna hesitates, still avoiding eye contact. 'Nnn…no,' she is shaking her head.

'Why not?'

'I-I-I have no….no friends, and my English not good.'

'It's all right. I will be your friend,' Dimple says. 'You seem to have difficulty when speaking, too?'

'Yes…ss,' Iryna looks tearful.

Dimple nods towards her friends. 'Don't worry, I have friends who stammer too,' She waves and invites them to join her and Iryna. The three give her quizzical looks, and then they squeeze together on one side of the table, ignoring the space beside Dimple and Iryna.

The other students in the canteen are busy eating, chatting, and making a lot of noise in the background. A girl walks in, and a boy at the end of the hall wolf-whistles. The other boys chuckle loudly. Everyone follows the boy's eyes, but the unintimidated girl rolls her eyes at the boy before joining the queue. A prefect walks over and tells the boys off, and the girls cheer by clapping.

'Hey, girls,' Dimple says. 'This is Iryna. She is new to Year 9, just like us. Iryna, meet Sophia.'

'Hi,' Sophia says.

'This is Jane.'

Jane says hello.

'And finally….'

'Hi, Iryna, my name is Tamara,' Tamara butts in. 'I think we are in the same form, am I correct?'

'Y…yes,' Iryna replies, shuffling her feet, clearly embarrassed about her speech impediment.

'Iryna is quite shy, and she has a little stammer,' Dimple points out to the other girls.

You can hear the clutter of cutlery and plates as the kitchen staff serves the students in the queue.

'Oi! You jumped the queue!' One boy says to another.

'Give us a chance,' the offending boy says. 'You were busy looking at the girls!'

There is laughter from others in the queue.

'So, you're not a show-off?' Jane asks Iryna.

Iryna shakes her head, sipping some water to calm her nerves.

Sophia puts a reassuring hand on her shoulder. 'Sorry, we misjudged you.'

'Yeah, me too,' Jane and Tamara say, one after the other.

Iryna is happy to have some friends at last! *Perhaps things will be fine after all.*

'Where do you live?' Dimple asks.

'F…four F…For…tttune Road (4, Fortune Road), with my mum and our English hosts – Ffreedddd and Jjjocelyn (Fred and Jocelyn).'

'Oh! I live at The Coppins, around the corner from you.' Dimple says. 'Do you know where that is?'

Iryna shakes her head.

'We are all your friends from now on,' Tamara says. Jane and Sophia nod.

The bell rings, signalling the end of the lunch period. The five girls walk toward the middle exit together, talking and laughing as they return to the classrooms.

❋ ❋ ❋ ❋ ❋ ❋ ❋ ❋ ❋

At home after school, Dimple tells Mum and Nana about Iryna and her stammer.

The Robinson women are all in the living room after dinner. Nana settles in her favourite armchair with a glass of wine. Mum sips tea while Dimple scoops strawberry ice cream out of a tub using a wooden spoon.

'I'm proud of you for making friends with Iryna,' Mum tells Dimple.

'Yes, Iryna is lovely. She is very neat, and her uniform is perfect. I can't imagine how she copes in a foreign country with the rest of her family in another nation. How can I help her, Mum? She is shy and scared to make friends because of her stammer.'

'It's quite easy, love. She has a condition called a 'speech block', Mum replies using air quotes. 'This happens when you try to hide an involuntary disruption in the flow of speech on certain sounds. Listen attentively when she speaks without 'helpful' interruptions and encourage her to be open about her stammer. You can also mention it to your teacher privately as she will know how best to support Iryna.'

'She doesn't live far from us,' Dimple adds.

'We could invite her to tea one of these days, then,' Mum says thoughtfully. 'Who does she live with?'

'Her mum and their English hosts. Iryna and her mum met Fred and Jocelyn at the airport when they arrived in the UK under the Homes for Affected Countries scheme.'

'I will invite them over soon,' Mum promises. 'I will also make enquiries at work to see if any services are available to help them.'

'I'm sure your school will have the right contacts to help Iryna once they know of her disability,' Nana says. 'Your grandad had a slight stammer when I first met him, but he learned to speak slowly, and I helped him build his confidence. We did not have the opportunities available these days, so we had to develop and work on a coping mechanism together.'

'I remember that, but he eventually stopped,' Mum says. 'I honestly can't remember the exact time it happened.'

'That's Nana's magic touch, I guess,' Dimple says proudly. 'I don't remember much about Grandad anymore.'

'He was a good man, very funny but equally hardworking,' Mum smiles as she reminisces about Grandad. 'He would often sing in the shower, "London bridge is falling down, falling down, falling down, London bridge is falling down, my fair lady!"'

Nana laughs at Mum's singing, thinking, *Joe Biden did grow up with a stammer, but his determination and perseverance propelled him to fame, and he became the 46th president of the United States of America.*

'Why don't we invite Iryna and her family to dinner?' Dimple asks.

'That's a bright idea, love,' Mum replies.

Dimple nods. 'Nai,' she says, recalling her Greek holiday with Mum in 2019, where they learned that *Nai* means Yes in Greek.

CHAPTER 5

> ✤ <

English Essay Contest

Miss Brown has given Year 9 an English essay. It is also a competition with a prize for the best essay.

Miss Brown's teaching method is technology-based, with online courses and resources to help the pupils. Each child has an iPad, which they can take home after classes. The pupils are to charge the iPad and remember to take it to school every day.

The essay topic is: *What do you want to do after your GCSEs?*

Dimple is reading her essay aloud in front of her bedroom mirror. With her hairbrush in hand, she pretends it is a microphone. She is waving her hands as though speaking in front of an audience. Kitty is on the floor by her side, trying to figure out what Dimple is doing. Miss Isabella has said it is good practice to read your essay aloud to give you confidence in what you have written.

After my GCSEs, I want to train to be a nurse, like my Mum and Grandma. I want to go into nursing to care for the sick and injured.

- *I remember how hard Mum worked to make people feel better during the Covid-19 pandemic.*
- *I remember clapping for the NHS staff on Thursday nights at 8pm.*
- *I remember watching Prime Minister Boris Johnson on the television screen thanking the NHS nurses for saving his life during the pandemic.*

My mother, Gloria, is a descendant of the Windrush generation. My grandmother, whom I fondly call Nana, came to England on a ship called the HMT Empire Windrush, which became a symbol of a wider mass migration movement.

In 1948, people from the Caribbean were invited to the UK to help rebuild post-war Britain, and many became nurses in the newly established NHS. This period known as the Windrush Era.

Before then, Florence Nightingale (the famous nurse known as 'The Lady with the Lamp) opened her first nursing school in the 1860s, and for the first time, consideration was given to the practical aspects of a nurse's uniform. Nurses should take pride in their appearance and maintain strict cleanliness and tidiness.

Coincidentally, in 1948, which was The Windrush year, the NHS was also founded, and part of that process was a new standard uniform consisting of a short-sleeved blue gown and a white apron with a red cross on it. Nowadays, nurses' uniforms have completely changed from large gowns and 'fever-proof dresses' to coloured scrubs and machine-washable fabrics, reflecting changes in technology and fashion. The uniforms are available in assorted colours, representing different specialisms or sectors within the NHS.'

I love my Mum's blue scrubs (top and trousers). The v-neckline and short-sleeved top has a small pocket on the right side. Of course, other nurses wear different uniforms, like Honey's traditional turquoise and white dress underneath a white apron and her starched, solid white traditional hat with decorative stitching.

The subjects I need to be a nurse include at least two (usually three) A-levels or equivalent qualifications at level 3, such as a T-level or BTECs, plus supporting GCSEs including English, maths and one science subject (usually biology or human biology).

I can also earn some money while I learn on the job and gain valuable life experience while working and training on the ward.

I have the qualities required to be a nurse because I am kind and love looking after people. Doing Mable's weekly shopping with Mum during the COVID-19 pandemic gave me great satisfaction.

I love looking after my poodle, Kitty, and I know they have dog therapy sessions for patients. I have heard Mum talk about the 'Meet Pets as Therapy.' (PAT).

Aside from my mum and my Nana, my nursing hero is Mary Jane Seacole, who helped the sick and wounded during the Crimean War (Mary picked up her nursing and healing skills from her mother, just as I hope to do) and finally, Lady Victoria Starmer, the new UK Prime Minister's wife, who works in occupational health within the NHS.

'What do you think of my essay?' Dimple asks Kitty.

Kitty wags her tail in approval.

'Come, let's go and find the rest of the family so I can see what they think of my essay.'

Kitty leads the way down the carpeted stairway.

'Mum, Nana, can I read my English essay to you?' Dimple asks as she enters the living room.

Without waiting for a response, she puts her hairbrush to her mouth and starts reading aloud to her Mum and Nana:

'After my GCSEs, I want to train to be a nurse, like my Mum and Grandma... and finally, Lady Victoria Starmer, the new UK Prime Minister's wife, who works in occupational health within the NHS.'

'That brought joyful tears to my eyes,' Nana says, applauding as Dimple finishes reading.

Mum is also clapping. 'I couldn't agree more.'

'I am so proud of you, Dimple,' Nana says. When Sally and I visited St Thomas Hospital during the pandemic, we saw Mary Seacole's statue, the first named memorial statue of a black woman in the UK. Mary was a British Jamaican nurse who cared for the injured British soldiers during the Crimean War. She was awarded the Jamaican Order of Merit in 1991.

'That is a good essay, Dimple,' Mum says. 'I am sure you will earn good marks when you submit it.

'When I started working as a nurse,' Nana continues, 'my Irish Nigerian colleague called Elizabeth, who is now known as RCN Fellow Dame Elizabeth Anionwu, was the first UK sickle-cell and thalassaemia specialist nurse. In 2018, during the NHS' 70th Anniversary celebrations, Elizabeth was listed among the 70 most influential nurses and midwives in history. She was also presented with a lifetime achievement award at the Daily Mirror's Pride of Britain Awards.'

'How cool is that!' Dimple says. 'Are you still in touch with her?'

'Not anymore,' Nana replies. 'Gloria, you can arrange for Dimple to do some work experience in your hospital, can't you?'

'Of course,' Mum replies. 'I will look into doing that for my Princess.'

'Did you also know that a lock of Florence Nightingale's hair from 1883 very recently made £2,800 at auction in Leyburn, North Yorkshire?'

'Where do you get all this information from, Nana?' Dimple asks.

'I read that in a newspaper. You must read, listen to the news and be aware of what is happening around you.'

'Every day is a school day,' Mum concludes.

CHAPTER 6

> ❄ <

Adam Gets a Provisional Driving Licence

Dad's study, the smallest room in the house, is adjacent to Adam's. A family picture of Dad, Mum, Adam, and Dimple is on the light blue wall above Dad's headrest.

'Knock, knock!' Adam enters.

Dad is busy on his laptop on a large wooden table in the middle of the room. There is a photocopier on the table. The blue décor gives the room a masculine touch. There is a bottle-fed water cooler in the corner of the room *and* a wastepaper basket by the desk. He looks up, carefully places his glasses on the desk and swirls his chair to the right in Adam's direction.

Adam picks up a photo frame on the edge of the table. 'Nana looks elegant in this photo.'

'To what do I owe the honour of this visit from my son?'

'Dad, you're talking as If I never come to say hello to you.'

'Only when you want something or need money.'

'No, Dad. I'm not here for money.'

'Really? Then what can I do you for? Or have you come to give me some of your money?'

'No, I'm here to spend quality time with my dad. Would you like some coffee?'

'Yes, please,' Dad smiles to himself. *Adam is up to something.*

'One coffee coming up!' Adam walks over to Dad's coffee machine beside the water cooler. He adds water to the water reservoir, inserts a filter, and adds coffee grounds before turning on the machine to brew.

Dad watches Adam out of the corner of his eye, then looks at the document he is holding as Adam returns to sit opposite him, shuffling his feet.

Dad pretends not to notice.

Adam coughs, clears his throat, and blurts out, 'Dad, will you teach me how to drive?'

'Ha, ha, ha! I knew you had something in mind,' Dad says. 'Where did this interest come from?'

'Well, I applied for my provisional licence, which came in the post the other day. Driving lessons are so expensive, so it would cost less and save us time if you could teach me in your spare time.'

Dad laughs and points at his son. 'By 'us', you mean Adam Robinson?'

'If I pass my test, you won't have to pick me up from the station anymore, and I can also drive Nana to her favourite places.'

'Well…. since you mentioned Nana, I'll think about it.'

Just then, Dimple enters the study. 'I thought I saw Adam coming over here. What does he want this time, Dad?'

'I came to remind Dad to have a break. I even made him coffee.'

'Yeah, right. Why did you really come over?'

'If you must know, I now have my provisional driver's licence and 'my dad' (pointing to dad) is going to give me extra driving lessons.'

'Is that true, Dad? You always do everything Adam asks.'

'I haven't made any promises, but I will see what I can do.

Dimple flashes her famous dimple. 'Alright, Dad, my turn!'

Dad places his document inside a folder on the table. 'I can see I won't get far with this paper.'

'I was thinking of the hospital placement Mum is arranging for me. Do you know what I'll be doing?'

'Your mum is the best person to discuss that with, love. If you have an idea of what you want and where your dream lies, that will help Mum organise the placement. Go with your heart, dear.'

'I would love to work with children,' Dimple says thoughtfully. 'I think they will be easier to care for.'

'Not necessarily,' Dad replies, 'but if you prefer to work in a children's ward, tell Mum as soon as possible.'

'Here, Dad,' Adam brings the coffee in a mug.

'How are you enjoying your mug, Dad?' Dimple asks.

Dad reads the imprint: '*El Sueno*'. 'This gift from your last holiday with Mum is a keeper. Thank you, young man.' He says to Adam. 'Have you decided between military training and University?'

'I think I will go to university, but I will take a gap year to attend military school.'

'That sounds like a good plan,' Dad says. *"The journey of a thousand miles begins with a single step."* You should draft your personal statement, explaining your interest in your chosen course, relevant skills, and life experiences.'

'Do you still want to study Psychology?' Dimple asks.

'Yep.'

'Remember to include your voluntary work during Covid and your part-time job during the holidays,' Dad says. 'And don't forget to emphasise why you have chosen Birmingham University.'

'Thanks, Dad. So, when are we starting the driving lessons?'

'Register with a driving school first, then I can help you with additional lessons as you progress.'

'The first single step for you, Adam,' Dimple says, imitating Dad's voice, 'is to register with a driving school.'

'What car do you think Dad will buy me when I go to Uni?' Adam asks with a wink.

'You'll be lucky!' Dimple says.

'There's no harm in dreaming ahead and hoping for a smooth four-wheel ride on campus.'

'The only smooth ride you will get from me is a lift to Uni on your first day!' Dad says. 'Then you're on your own, young man!'

'You seriously don't mean that, Dad.'

'Yes, he does,' Dimple says.

Dad points to a poster behind his desk. 'See these two great men? In 1963, the guy to the left, Martin Luther King, made a famous speech:

"I have a dream that my four little children will one day live in a nation where they will not be judged by the colour of their skin but by the content of their character. I have a dream today!"

He had a vision where people can achieve their dreams regardless of race or background.'

'… and Obama became the 1st Black President of the United States of America,' Adam concludes.

'Exactly, I'm glad you're getting my point.' Dad says, smiling.

'I'm proud of you for getting your provisional licence,' Dimple tells her brother.

'Thanks, Sis,' Adam replies with a wink.

'Now, if you two will excuse me, I need to get back to work.' Dad says.

CHAPTER 7

>❋<

English Essay Results

Mr Cipolla is on stage addressing the students at the Assembly Hall.

'I'm glad you have welcomed our new students to the school. There has been helpful feedback from parents that their wards feel welcome and supported to pursue their educational journeys within our school walls. Remember to sign up for the after-school activities to enrich your learning and provide opportunities to make friends outside your immediate group.'

'Besides the Red Cross and language clubs, we have added netball to this year's sports activities. The netball court is off-site, but this should not put you off signing up. There is also a new club – The African Caribbean Society – where you can learn about other cultures. Lastly, I would like to invite Miss Brown to the stage to announce the Year 9 essay competition results.'

The students murmur loudly as Miss Brown walks up the stage.

'Hush!' Mr Cipolla cautions, 'or we will not hear the results.' He passes the microphone to Miss Brown.

'Good morning, school.' She begins.

'Good morning, Miss Brown!' the students chorus.

'Last week, I asked Year 9 students to write an essay about the career they would like to take up after leaving school, to which we had answers like being journalists, doctors, scientists, and lawyers. Some were not sure what they would like to do, and that is also fine. The exercise was to get them and everyone in this room thinking about the future and how to go about making your dreams possible. I'm surprised no one wants to be an English teacher!' (laughter from the whole hall).

'I have marked the essays, and Mr Cipolla agrees with my decision. Joint first prize goes to Dimple Robinson and Iryna Braverman.'

A round of applause fills the hall.

'Like her mum and nana, Dimple would like to be a nurse because she wants to help people and save lives,' Miss Brown continues, 'Dimple's empathy and commitment is transparent throughout her essay. She talked fondly of the National Health Service from observing her mum at work during the Covid era.

'Iryna is a new student seeking asylum in England, away from the war in her country. Many fled neighbouring war-torn European countries, and some now live with generous host families. It is difficult for these families to leave everything familiar behind and start new lives abroad. When she first arrived, Iryna could not speak any English, but she quickly picked up the language with her foster parents' help. Her new friendship with Dimple added to her confidence. In her essay, Iryna talks about her country's rich heritage and her dream to be a lawyer so she can be an advocate for the less privileged. Girls, come up and collect your prizes from Mr Cipolla.'

The headteacher walks back to the centre of the stage and presents both girls with vouchers towards their chosen after-school activities.

❋❋❋❋❋❋❋❋❋

'Dimple is doing everything with Iryna now,' Jane whispers to Tamara and Sophia.

'I agree,' Tamara replies, 'she doesn't spend as much time with us as before.'

'They live near each other,' Sophia adds. 'So they see each other over the weekends, too.'

'Hush!' the Head of Year says to the girls, putting a finger to her lips.

They stop whispering, and Sophia watches the other two girls look on jealously as Dimple and Iryna collect their vouchers.

The school bell rings. The teachers walk out of the assembly hall, and the students follow the usual procedure.

Dimple and her friends walk into their classroom.

'PE is today's first subject,' Jane announces. 'I'm going to the changing room.'

Tamara grabs her bag from her locker. 'Wait for me!'

'Hold on, Iryna and I are coming too,' Dimple says.

By the time Dimple gets out her PE kit, Jane and Tamara have disappeared.

'Iryna, let's go and join them on the sports ground. Hey, you didn't wait for us!' She says to Jane and Tamara.

Without a word, the two girls move to another area of the ground.

'Sophia, what's the matter with them?' Dimple asks.

'I don't know,' Sophia says, 'but I think they are peeved that they did not get a prize for the English essay.'

'Oh, I'm sorrrry,' Iryna says.

'You don't have to be sorry,' Sophia says, walking over to Tamara's side. (She is torn between her loyalty to Dimple and Tamara).

'Don't worry, Iryna, we deserve our prizes,' Dimple says. 'I just wish the other girls wouldn't behave so childishly.'

The Sports teacher blows his whistle, there is silence, and the class begins.

Dimple tries to catch her friends' attention, but they blank her.

'I don't want to come between you and your friends,' Iryna says.

'You are my friend, too,' Dimple says as they do their warmups. 'I'm sure they will cool down later. So, what will you spend your voucher on?'

'I haven't decided yet,' Iryna replies.

'I think I will join the First Aid class to learn what to do in an emergency medical situation.'

'I could come with you to that class,' Iryna says.

'It's settled then, we will tell Mr Cipolla tomorrow. Thank you for supporting me on this, Iryna.'

'You are welcome. I'm sure I will also learn from the lessons.'

CHAPTER 8

> ❀ ⟨

Iryna Comes to Dinner

It is a Saturday afternoon. Dimple knocks and then enters Nana's bedroom.

'Nana, Iryna and her family are coming over tonight for dinner.'

Nana is lying on her double bed watching a programme on the large-screen television. 'I know. We need to get dinner ready for them. Is your Mum awake after her late-night shift?'

'Yes, she said we should start, and she will join us in the kitchen soon.'

Nana switches off her TV, puts the remote control on her dressing table and leads the way to the kitchen. Dimple pulls down two aprons from behind the kitchen door. 'Here, Nana.

You said we could make the Platinum Jubilee cake for Iryna.' She hands over the brown apron and puts on the lilac one.

Nana wears the apron over her brown cowl-neck jumper and preheats the oven while they mix the ingredients. 'Exactly. We will give Iryna and her family a taste of the Jubilee celebrations.'

Dimple lays the ingredients on the table. She is keen to learn from her grandmother.

'Dimple, why do you bring a pudding to boil?' Nana asks.

'No idea, Nana.'

Mum walks in wearing an orange jumper. She selects a pink apron from the door rack, washes her hands at the sink and dries them with a tea towel.

'You bring a pudding to boil first to kill the enzymes in the eggs, so they don't eat the starch and make your pudding watery in the fridge,' Nana tells Dimple. 'You also add one egg at a time into the cake batter and blend each one.'

'I read that in the recipe book but didn't know the science behind it. I love you so much, Nana. You seem to know everything!'

'That's Nana for you,' Mum says.

'How was your shift last night, Gloria?' Nana asks.

'Quiet. A couple of new patients were admitted to the ward, which required closely examining their dispatch notes and getting to know them.'

Mum reaches for the kettle. 'Anyone for a cuppa? I'm making some tea.'

'Coffee for me, please,' Nana says, then she reads the recipe instructions. Dimple helps her prepare the batter. Mum hands Nana her coffee and takes a sip from her teacup. After what seems like a long time to Dimple, Mum places the mixture in the oven, turning the temperature to 180°C.

Dimple wipes her forehead with her grey jumper sleeve. 'I feel so hot!'

'Can you put the Swiss roll layer in the fridge, Dimple?' Mum asks.

'I sure can.' Dimple says and shuts the fridge door with a whomp! At the same time, Nana reaches for her half-finished cup of coffee.

Dad walks into the kitchen. 'What is that aroma tickling my taste buds?'

'We're making a cake for Iryna and her Mum's visit tonight,' Dimple says excitedly.

'What sort of cake is it?'

'A Lemon Swiss roll and amaretti trifle. We're replicating the Platinum Jubilee cake.'

'That's a warm gesture to welcome Iryna to the community,' Dad says. 'What time are we expecting them?'

'I told Iryna at school we would expect them at 7pm.'

'Yeah, that is a good time as it gets dark quickly now,' Mum says.

Just then, Adam enters the kitchen, and his glasses immediately fog up. 'What the heck,' he cries, taking off his glasses to wipe them.

'If you can't stand the heat, get out of the kitchen!' Dimple replies cheekily.

'Alright, Chef Dimple!' With that, Adam makes a quick exit.

'What do you think Iryna would like to eat?' Mum asks Dimple.

'She is not a fussy eater,' Dimple replies, 'and she loves to try new recipes.'

'We'll make jerk chicken and rice then,' Mum decides.

Dimple licks her lips. 'Ha, that's Nana's speciality!'

'We can have butternut and pumpkin soup for starters,' Nana adds.

Mum gets the chicken out, and Nana starts seasoning the pieces.

Dimple reaches for the rice bag in the cupboard. 'How many cups of rice do we need?'

'How many guests are we expecting?' Nana asks.

'Four – Iryna, her mum and the foster parents – plus the five of us, makes nine people in total.' Dimple says, counting on her fingers.

'Well, I'll make one cup per person but ten cups, as we can always leave the rest in the fridge.' Nana replies.

'Was nursing practised differently when you were working in Scotland, Nana?' Dimple asks.

'The level of care is the same in Scotland,' Nana replies. 'I worked for the NHS there, so it is the same as your mum's. I think nursing chooses you because it is not just a career. It is a calling.'

'I agree with Nana,' Mum adds. 'Nursing is a vocation that fills you with pride and satisfaction as the patients you look after feel better through your care. Nana, shall I start on the soup while you concentrate on the rice?'

'Yes, I've got this covered.' Nana says.

Dimple darts from one part of the kitchen to another, helping Mum and Nana.

'When I start working as a nurse, three generations of our family will be nurses.'

'That will bring me great joy,' Nana says, clapping her hands.

'Mum, we only have six dining chairs. How are we going to sit three extra people?'

'I can sit in my armchair,' Nana says. 'We will find a way.'

'When there's a will, there's a way,' Dimple mimics. She takes some plates and cutlery and heads to the dining area to set up the table.

'Where is Adam when you need his help?' Dimple says.

'Adam!' she shouts up the stairs.

No reply.

She shouts his name again.

'What do you want?' Adam yells from his bedroom.

'We need extra chairs for our guests at the dining table.'

'They're your guests, not mine!'

'That is not a nice thing to say to your sister!' Dad points out from his room.

'Alrlght then, how many more chairs do you need, Dimple?'

'Two chairs will be okay; Nana will sit in her armchair.'

Adam comes down the stairs with two chairs, puts them down and rushes back to his room.

Mum enters the dining area. 'The food is almost ready. Can we all start getting ready before our guests arrive?'

At 7 pm on the dot, the doorbell rings.

Dimple rushes to open the door, hugs Iryna and lets the guests in to the hall area. Kitty follows closely on her heels, wagging her tail as though curious to see who the guests are.

Mum comes towards the door. 'Hello, my name is Gloria. I'm Dimple's mum. Please hang up your coats on the rack by the door.'

Iryna, who walks in first, is startled as Kitty gets close and places her paws on Iryna's legs. She is unsure how to behave around Kitty.

'I hope you're not scared of dogs, Iryna?' Dimple asks. 'Kitty is a good dog.'

'Nice to meet you, Mrs Robinson,' Iryna says. 'I have heard so much about you.' She is wearing a pink jumper over blue jeans; her long brown hair is brushed into a ponytail.

'Good things, I hope?' Gloria says with a smile. She gestures toward the living room. 'Please come in, everyone.'

'Hello Gloria,' Jocelyn says. She is about five feet, six inches tall, wearing a black sweater over her grey blouse and purple trousers.

'Do you need us to take our shoes off?' Fred asks. Slightly shorter than his wife, he has a cheerful, friendly face. He is wearing a pair of glasses with thick black frames.

Dimple's dad gets up from the settee in the living room and holds out his hand to shake the guests. 'No, please just make yourself comfortable. I'm James, Dimple's dad. Please meet my Mum, Nana Patricia,' he points to Nana, 'and this is Dimple's brother Adam.'

Iryna's mum shakes hands with Dad. 'My name is Helena.'

'Oh! I see the resemblance.' Mum says. 'Like mother-like- daughter. Same hair and eyes.'

Everyone shakes hands before taking their seats.

Dad turns to Fred. 'How did you end up hosting Helena and Iryna?'

'We applied to be hosts and were paired up through the government website.' Fred replies.

'As soon as we saw Iryna's photograph, we knew we wanted to help her.' Jocelyn adds. 'Her dad and brother are still in their country, which is a big worry.'

'My English, not good,' Helena says. 'Thank you, Dimple, for helping Iryna.'

'I'm glad Dimple made friends with Iryna,' Mum says, leading the way to the dining room. 'Please come over to the dining table.' She and Nana then head into the kitchen.

Dimple sits next to Iryna while the others find chairs to sit on. Kitty sits on the floor by Dimple's legs, licking her lips.

As Mum and Nana return to the dining room carrying the soup, Iryna looks up excitedly.

'The soup smells nice,' Fred says.

'It's Nana's butternut and pumpkin soup,' Dimple offers.

'Where are you originally from?' Fred asks Nana.

'I came to this country to join my late husband, who had served in the British Navy,' Nana replies.

Mum starts to serve the soup in white bowls.

'I will help you, Mum,' Dimple gets up to pass the soup bowls around to everyone.

'My late husband arrived here in 1948, a year before me,' Nana continues.

'Is that part of the Windrush generation?' Jocelyn asks.

'Exactly. We settled in Scotland, where I worked as a nurse, and my husband worked in a factory.'

'Do you mind if we say the grace first?' Dad says.

Fred has just raised the soup spoon to his mouth, and he nearly chokes as he stops abruptly. He is clearly surprised at this request.

'Dimple, do you mind sharing the grace?' Dad asks.

Dimple says a short prayer, including a sentence for Iryna's dad and brother.

'Please have your soup before it gets cold,' Mum says.

'This tastes nice!' Helena says as she carefully puts a little spoonful into her mouth.

Mum passes her the breadbasket. 'Thank you.'

Helena takes a bread roll, passes the basket to Jocelyn, and it goes round to everyone on the table.

'The weather is changing, and it is getting dark early,' Dad says.

'Yes. Helena, Iryna and I went shopping for winter items last week,' Jocelyn says.

'Mum got me a nice navy-blue winter jacket, gloves and a pair of black boots,' Iryna says.

'What shop did you go to?' Dimple asks.

'Primark,' Iryna replies.

'I love Primark!' Dimple says. 'I will invite you when I go to the mall with my other friends.'

Mum returns to the kitchen. This time, Dimple follows her and helps put the food platters on the table.

Jocelyn inhales the smell. 'Wow! What food is this?'

'It's Nana's rice with jerk chicken,' Dimple says.

'Will you share the recipe with me later?' Jocelyn asks.

'That would be my pleasure,' Nana replies, passing the rice platter to Jocelyn.

Dad passes the chicken to Adam, who is sitting next to him.

'There is some salad over here,' Adam says, handing the bowl around.

Soon, everyone has full plates of food.

'What do you do, Gloria?' Jocelyn asks.

'I work as a nurse at the local hospital. Nana was a nurse before she retired, too.'

'So, nursing is in the family,' Fred says between mouthfuls. 'This chicken is delicious!'

'Iryna mentioned that Dimple wants to be a nurse, too,' Jocelyn says.

'Yes, 'Nana chips in. 'It was good to learn that both girls got joint-first position in their English essay.'

'Is the food okay, Helena?' Mum asks.

Helena nods and wipes her mouth with a table napkin. 'It is delicious, thank you.'

'Helena is taking English lessons at the community centre, one day a week,' Jocelyn says. 'Iryna attended some classes, but since she started school, she no longer needs those classes.'

'Yes, I can see that her English is good,' Dad says.

'Her English, better than mine,' Helena says proudly.

'So, what do you do for the rest of the week?' Mum asks Helena.

'I help in the school,' Helena says.

'She is a part-time classroom assistant at our local primary school,' Fred replies.

'St Peter's?' Nana asks.

'Yes.' Fred confirms.

'That's not far from my over-60s club, which is why I know it so well,' Nana explains.

'There is more food. Please help yourselves,' Dad offers, just as Dimple says, 'Nana plays the piano to her friends at the club!'

'Iryna is learning to play the piano, and Helena makes nice outfits,' Jocelyn says, looking impressed. 'She trained as a dressmaker in her country.'

'I will introduce you to my younger sister, Helena.' Gloria says warmly. 'Nadia is more outgoing than me, and she is always looking to make nice outfits.'

Helena thanks her quietly.

'And what does the young man do?' Fred asks.

'Me?' Adam is slightly surprised, as he has kept out of the conversations so far.

'Yes, you, young man.'

Dimple teases her brother. 'Young man, what do you do?'

'I'm in my last year of sixth form and planning to attend university next year,' Adam replies.

'That's good,' Fred says. 'You must have a goal to focus on.'

Nana interrupts the conversation. 'Who is up for dessert?'

'Oh, I'm stuffed already!' Jocelyn says.

'Ah, the women have saved the best dish for last,' Dad says proudly.

Nana sets off to bring in the pudding while Mum chats with Jocelyn and Helena. Dimple clears the table, and Iryna helps her take the dirty dishes to the kitchen. Just as the bell chimes on the living room television announce the nine o'clock news, Nana brings in the dessert on a silver tray, with Dimple and Iryna behind her, carrying the dessert plates and spoons, respectively.

Mum gets up to assist Nana. 'We made a replica of the lemon and Swiss roll Platinum Jubilee trifle for you,' she tells the guests.

Fred smiles. 'You have gone to great lengths to entertain us.'

'We will reciprocate your kindness by inviting you to ours as well,' Jocelyn says simultaneously.

Fred takes a bite and licks his spoon. 'This is utterly delicious!'

'Yes, I like it very much,' Helena says.

'What a delight,' Jocelyn adds.

'Is anyone a Royal fan, then?' Fred asks.

'Princess Diana was my favourite royal,' Mum replies. I have not followed them much since her death, to be honest.'

'I enjoyed watching the Jubilee celebrations on TV,' Nana puts in.

'We had a street party here that day,' Dad adds.

'Do you have a Royal family like ours, Helena?' Mum asks.

Helena shakes her head. 'No, we do not.'

The dinner party retires to the living room, carrying their drinks with them.

Fred rubs his stomach, sipping red wine from his glass. 'It's been such a lovely evening. Thanks again for inviting us.'

'Thank you for coming over,' James replies. 'I am glad we can finally spend time with you and get to know Iryna better.'

'Dimple speaks fondly of Iryna all the time,' Nana says.

'Dad, may I show Iryna my room, please?'

'Sure, you can.'

'Come with me, Iryna,' Dimple says to her friend. As they head upstairs, Adam seizes the opportunity to escape from the older company. Dimple opens the door to her room, and Iryna walks in with Kitty on her heels.

'Wow, your room is big and beautiful!' Iryna gasps, taking in the lilac-coloured room and furniture.

Dimple thanks her.

'Who is wearing a nurse's uniform in the photo on your dressing table?'

'That is my mum when she first started nursing, long before I was born. She looks different in that picture since she was much younger.'

'I see why you want to be a nurse, Dimple. Your mum is so pretty.'

'Thanks.' Dimple says.

✱ ✱ ✱ ✱ ✱ ✱ ✱ ✱

Downstairs, the adults are still talking.

'So, what do you both do now?' Dad asks the guests.

'Fred and I are newly retired,' Jocelyn replies.

'We run an after-school club at St. Peter's, which is how we got Helena a job at the school,' Fred adds.

'That's handy!' Nana says, smiling broadly. 'You could join in the activities at our over-60s club when you have the time if you like.'

'That would be nice,' Jocelyn replies, 'Is the club free to join?'

'Yes, it is run by the council.'

Dad turns on the TV with the remote control. 'Shall we see what programme is on the telly?'

'…. *Celebrity Catchphrase*, *A Tribute to ABBA*…, there isn't much choice on the telly nowadays. What should we watch?'

'We can watch *Celebrity Catchphrase*,' Jocelyn says.

'Lingo is Iryna's favourite programme,' Fred says. 'It is such a special show for us at home.'

'A real test of who can shout at the telly the loudest!' Jocelyn chuckles.

'I don't think I've seen that programme,' Dad says.

'In the show, three pairs of contestants go head-to-head, in a battle of words. They must correctly and quickly work out the words that appear in the Lingo grid.

The Lingo computer gives contestants the first letter of different length words. The contestants have to think quickly. If they correctly guess the word, they'll bank money and increase their potential winnings,' Fred explains.

'It has helped Iryna with her English,' Helena adds. 'I find it too difficult.'

'And improved her confidence while speaking,' Jocelyn adds.

Nana gets up – 'Tea or coffee, anyone?'

'Oh, no. I am full up, thank you,' Helena rubs her belly.

'Same here,' Fred and Jocelyn say together, shaking their heads.

Mum goes to the bottom of the stairs. 'Dimple! Come down now. It is time for your friend to go home.'

Upstairs, Dimple hands Iryna a black cotton bag. 'Coming, Mum!'

'What's in it?' Her friend opens the bag containing clothes and a pair of shoes. She looks at Dimple in amazement.

'Mum said I could give you some of my clothes as we are the same size,' Dimple says.

'Thank you, Dimple!' Iryna grabs her friend in a warm embrace before rushing downstairs, taking two steps at a time.

'Mum! Look! Dimple gave me some of her clothes and this brown teddy bear.'

'That is kind. Thank you,' Helena says to Dimple.

'They are not all new items, but Dimple wanted to share some of her stuff with her friend,' Mum says.

The guests move towards the front door.

'Here, let me see If I can identify your coats,' Dad offers.

'The long, black woollen coat is Fred's,' Iryna says.

'And I think the brown fleece jacket belongs to Iryna's mum?' Dimple asks.

'Correct,' Iryna says, 'and the yellow jacket is mine, thank you.'

'Then this grey puffer one must belong to Jocelyn,' Dad concludes.

'Thank you for such a warm welcome,' Jocelyn says as Fred drapes the coat over her shoulders, checking that the buttons are fastened correctly.

'And for the lovely dinner,' he adds, rubbing his hands together in delight.

'I will send you the recipe through Dimple on Monday,' Nana tells Jocelyn.

Dimple opens the front door. 'Goodnight, Iryna.'

'Oh dear!' Iryna gasps as the cold breeze blows her hair in all directions.

'Pull your scarf tightly around your neck, Iryna,' Dimple instructs.

'Thank you. See you at school on Monday,' Iryna says before braving herself for the journey home.

CHAPTER 9

➤❀❧

Work Experience at the Hospital
– Day 1

'Hi Sophia! Hi Iryna! I'm glad you could join me on this video call so early. I'm nervous about starting at the hospital today.'

'You've got this,' Sophia says.

You are lucky your mum works in the same hospital,' Iryna adds. 'I think the staff will look after you.'

'I've got a big knot in my stomach, but I am also looking forward to the day.'

'Have faith in yourself, Dimple,' Sohpia assures her.

'Dimple, are you ready?' Mum yells across the first-floor landing. 'You will end up catching the bus if you aren't ready by the time I get to my car.'

'Remember our first aid training,' Iryna continues, 'practice taking deep breaths.'

'Dimple!!!' Mum shouts again.

'Alright, Mum. I'm coming downstairs now.'

'I think she is on her phone again,' Nana's voice can be heard in the living room. 'These children are always bent over their phones. The screen is not good for their eyes, but they don't listen to an experienced woman like me. Dimple, you don't want to be late on your first day at work!'

'It's not as though I will be paid, Nana. It's just work experience.' Dimple shouts back. 'I am getting my backpack now.'

Dimple bends down to put on her shoes, whispering to her friends, 'All right, girls. I've got to go. Wish me luck, and I'll tell you about my first day later.'

'Bye, Dimple!' Iryna and Sophia say together.

Dimple gets into the car, and Mum drives to the hospital. It's a warm Monday morning on the first of her seven-day work experience. When Dad asked Dimple where she would like to work, she did not think twice.

'A hospital!' she replied excitedly.

Mum then spoke to Matron in her ward, who agreed that Dimple could work in a different ward at the same hospital.

Dimple takes in the sights as Mum drives through the hospital gates. Two car parks, one marked for staff use and the other for visitors, are to their left. Mum drives slowly through the grounds towards the main entrance door. At the end of the long road, she turns into the car park, where Dimple notices a sign for the paediatric section. Mum drives past the barriers to the staff car park, notices a vacant bay and pulls in. They cross the zebra crossing to the main hospital entrance.

Next to the entrance is the Accident and Emergency (A&E) department, where three ambulances are parked. Although several cars pull up, they only drop off patients as no one can park in front of the hospital. Dimple walks behind Mum through the revolving doors, presses the sanitiser button, rubs the gel on her hands, and then follows Mum to the reception desk on the left.

Two ladies in striped blue and white uniforms welcome them with nice smiles.

'Didn't I see you yesterday, Gloria?' Martha says with a smile.

'Nope, that was a long Friday ago!' Mum says as they approach the reception desk. 'Dimple, you remember Martha and Amber?' She gives them both a wave.

'Gloria, it's great to see you and… Is this young Dimple?' Amber sounds startled. 'My, oh my! Hasn't she grown since I saw her last?'

'Thank you, Amber,' Mum says. 'It's her first day of work experience. She will be in Judith's charge.'

Dimple smiles, revealing her dimple. 'Good morning,' She says to both ladies before walking slightly ahead of Mum, feeling self-conscious and somewhat nervous about the day ahead.

Mum walks past the reception desk and turns left past a chemist, where there is a short queue. The supermarket opposite is full of people buying various items. They walk up to the first floor, through the visitor's lounge, to access the ward using her staff pass.

At the end of the corridor, she opens the door to Matron's office and peeps in. Judith, the matron, is there. Her red hair ties into a bun at the top of her head.

'Good morning, Gloria.' She says, 'Hello, Dimple. Are you ready for your first day?'

'Good morning, Judith. Yes, I am,' Dimple says politely.

'Right, Matron. I will leave Dimple with you while I start my shift in the Green Ward. See you after work, daughter. Call me when you are finished for the day.'

'Thanks, Mum. See you later.'

'Take a seat, young lady,' Judith says as Mum closes the door behind her. 'Would you like a cup of tea or hot chocolate before I introduce you to your mentor?'

'I'm fine, thank you,' Dimple replies. 'My Nana made sure I had breakfast before leaving home.'

'Very well, follow me. I will introduce you to Laura, who will oversee your training.'

Judith exits her office and turns left to the next room. 'Hi Laura, Dimple is here. I am sure she will enjoy shadowing you in your duties.'

Laura has medium-length blonde hair, which falls just short above her shoulders.

She gets up to shake Dimple's hand. 'Hi, I'm Laura, and I will be your mentor for the week.'

'Hi Laura, thank you for having me.'

'Let me know if you need anything else,' Matron tells Dimple before leaving the room.

'We have to sort out your uniform first,' Laura says. 'Come with me.' They walk over to take the Goods lift to the ground floor. A male and female staff member sit at separate desks in the administrative office.

'Hi, Dan. I believe you have uniforms and a name badge for Dimple, our work experience candidate?'

'What dress size are you, Dimple?' Dan asks, scrutinising the uniform piles on the table.

'I am a regular size 8,' Dimple answers.

'You will need trousers, shirts, a fleece, and your name badge,' Dan says, packing some clothes into a small blue bag. 'Okay. Some of our regular sizes may be a bit big,' he continues, 'If there are problems with any item, please come back to me.'

Laura thanks him before looking inside the bag. She reads out the name on the badge, checking for spelling errors. In the general staff room, Laura hands Dimple the bag and points to the Ladies.

'You can change into your uniform in there.'

A few minutes later, Dimple is wearing a white, short-sleeved cotton shirt with buttons from top to bottom. The shirt has two front pockets and blue trimmings around the collar and sleeves. She teams this up with navy-wide trousers. However, she keeps fidgeting with the waist, buttoning and unbuttoning her top to reassure herself that it is the right fit.

'Don't worry, you will get used to the uniform.' Laura assures her before giving Dimple a brief introduction to the ward. The Rainbow Children's Unit has 27 children with several conditions and illnesses and is split into three areas: Red, Yellow, and Blue.

'The doctors do ward rounds to see every patient between 8 and 9am.' She explains. 'Then, between nine and eleven, the nursing assistants wash the children's hair, clean their teeth, and provide other personal care, and the children have breakfast and get ready for the day. During the day, depending on their fitness levels, they do different activities, including painting, IT exercises and music sessions. Let me take you for a walk round the ward.'

Dimple meets dieticians, physiotherapists, psychologists, pharmacists, and doctors who are busy working. On returning to the staff room, she makes a mental note of the offices, where Laura gives Dimple a break for tea and biscuits.

'I think you've done enough for one day, Dimple,' Laura says. 'Tomorrow, we will familiarise you with the ward equipment. If you have any questions, you can come with them tomorrow.'

'Thank you,' Dimple says before phoning to let Mum know she is finished for the day.

'How was your first day?' Mum asks as she turns on the ignition key.

'Everybody was helpful, but there are many things to learn.'

'Like what?'

'The different types of equipment and getting to know each patient individually.'

'…And why are you cradling your head in your hand?'

'My head is spinning after so much information.'

'This is only day one, mind you,' Mum remarks.

'I know.'

'It will get better, don't worry,' Mum says sympathetically, pulling up outside the house. 'Here you go, I'm not coming inside. Say hello to Nana.'

'Thank you, Mum.'

Mum drives off into the distance.

Dimple lets herself into the house with her keys. 'Hello, Nana!'

'What are you cooking, Nana?' Dimple asks as she inhales the aroma of food coming from the kitchen.

'How are you, Pet? Did you enjoy your first day?'

'Yes, Nana. It was okay. I will be working at The Rainbow Unit on the children's ward.'

'That is good,' Nana says. 'I was about to set the table. I made some macaroni cheese for dinner.'

Dimple kneels to give Kitty a scratch under her tummy. 'I'll take my bag upstairs and then come and help you, Nana. Kitty, let's take my bag to my room, then we'll come down to help.' The dog opens her mouth and jumps at Dimple's knee.

'Nana, the food smells nice,' Dimple says when she enters the kitchen minutes later. 'How many people are having dinner? Is Adam at home yet?'

Nana shrugs. 'I haven't seen him.'

'It's just you, me and Kitty, then,' Dimple says, skipping around the table. 'Two plates, two sets of cutlery, and two glasses on the table. Nice and easy! Now, Kitty, here's your food in your bowl. Be a good girl, and do not gobble it all at once!'

Nana sits opposite Dimple. 'So, tell me more about your day.'

'I was introduced to many people, mostly staff, but I cannot remember everyone's names.'

'You will by the end of the week, I assure you,' Nana replies.

'There is a day room with a small TV, a microwave and a fridge where we can eat lunch,' Dimple continues. 'I will find out more tomorrow.'

'Try and have a good night's kip, dear.'

'I will. Thanks Nana.'

Work Experience at the Hospital – Day 2

Dimple wakes up early, gets showered and dressed in her uniform before heading for the dining room where Nana is waiting.

'What would you like for breakfast?'

'Oats and pancakes, please.'

'Coming up, Princess!' Nana says, heading for the kitchen. Dimple follows her.

'You are not coming into the kitchen in your nice white shirt!' Nana tells her. 'Go back; Nana will look after you today.'

'Yes, Super Nana!' Dimple says, returning to the dining room.

Dad comes down the stairs, says, 'Hello, Dimple!' and enters the kitchen.

He envelopes Nana in a big hug. 'Morning, Mum.'

'Morning, love. Would you like something to eat?'

'Could do. I'm not due at work early today. What's Dimple having?'

'Oats and pancakes!' Dimple hollers.

'I'll have the same.'

'Coming right up!' Nana chirps.

'Thank you, Chef.' Dad goes to sit with Dimple. 'Are you looking forward to your second day at the hospital, love?'

'Yes, Dad. Everyone is lovely and nice to me. I can't wait to get to know the children in the ward.'

Dad ruffles Dimple's hair. 'That's my girl! Remember to switch your phone off, though. I know you like catching up with your friends.'

'I leave my personal belongings, including my phone, in a locker in the female changing room.'

'Alright then,' Dad replies. 'You must give the patients your undivided attention at all times.'

Mum is coming down from her bedroom. 'That is true.' She enters the kitchen, makes some coffee, and gives Nana a quick hug.

'Are you having breakfast, Gloria?'

'No, thanks. Just coffee and a packed lunch.'

Mum and Nana get busy. Nana makes breakfast for everyone, and Mum prepares packed lunches for herself, Dad, and Dimple. Nana puts the food on the table and Dimple and Dad help themselves.

'Dad, pass me the syrup, please.' Dimple collects the bottle from Dad and squirts syrup over her pancakes.

Dad adds honey to his oats. 'This is lovely. Thank you, Nana.'

'That's okay, love. You're not too old for me to feed, and you work extremely hard. You need looking after too.'

'Nana, you spoil us all!' Dimple says.

'Young lady, don't take too long eating,' Mum says to her daughter, then turns to Dad. 'Are you working late today, James?'

'Yes. I have a late start. Hopefully, there won't be too many emergencies, so I can finish yesterday's reports. What about you?'

'I'm on flexible shifts this week, so I can drop off and bring Dimple home after her shifts.'

'Thank you for arranging that.'

'Not a problem,' Mum says, 'I have two night shifts, though.'

'I can always pick Dimple up if you need me to,' Nana offers.

'Thanks, Nana. I will bear that in mind. I think I've got it covered for now.'

Mum and Dimple leave the house and walk towards the car in front of the house. Dimple looks through yesterday's notes on the drive. The weather is warm but not sunny, and the traffic is light. Mum wades through the usual route to the hospital and parks up. This time, Dimple leads the way to the main entrance. The ladies at the reception are busy today, so Mum walks Dimple straight to Rainbow Ward and leaves her in the staff room. Dimple enters the female changing room, places her backpack in a middle locker and pins the locker key to her left front pocket.

Laura is at the ward reception desk, talking to one of the relatives.

'Hi Laura, how was your daughter when you got home yesterday?' Dimple asks.

'Sara was fine, thank you. Her dad picked her up from nursery, and she was fed washed and ready for bed by the time I got home.

'I hope I get to see her before I leave.'

'I'm sure you will. It's nice to see you again, Dimple. I see I did not scare you off with my talking yesterday?'

'Oh, you didn't. I told Nana all about you and the ward when I got home.'

'Positive things, I hope?'

'Of course. She liked my uniform too; she said I looked smart and professional.'

'I will show you our stock room. It's over this way.' Laura points ahead, and they walk towards the room. 'You can get anything you need for work here.'

Dimple nods. 'They are nicely stacked in different sections.'

'You need an orderly system to work in a busy ward like ours. Over on this side is the stack of machines we use.' Laura taps a machine to her left. 'To measure the amount of glucose in the blood, you place a drop of blood from a fingerstick on a test strip, which is then inserted into the meter.'

'What is the machine called?'

'A Glucometer.' Laura replies. 'In addition, hoists, slings, and other moving and handling aids remove the need for manual lifting, so hospitals, nursing homes, and community staff no longer need to lift patients.

'This, here, is the vital observation machine. As you can see, it is a portable device that collects the patient's real-time data. Are you ready to do the rounds with me to observe how we use some of the equipment?'

* * * * * * * * *

This morning, the matron admitted a new patient to the ward, and Laura spends the break going through her admission notes.

Aisha, a nine-year-old girl who was bitten by a dog while in the park with her dad and brother, has been transferred from A&E. They spent four hours in A&E before being seen by a doctor. After the initial treatment, which included a tetanus injection, she was transferred to The Rainbow ward for overnight observation.

When Dimple returns, Laura leads her to Room 2A, Aisha's room. As they walk along the white corridors, Dimple notices the framed yellow and orange pictures of a giraffe, tiger, crocodile, and photographs of young children. The soft colours brighten the corridor passage.

Room 2A, the first room on the left, has three beds. The bedding and walls are white, but a picture of a rainbow hangs at the far end. A small television is in the centre of the room. Laura walks up to the first bed on the right.

Aisha is lying on the single bed, her head on a pillow. She is wearing pink pyjamas, and her dark-brown hair is held with a pink bandana. Next to her bed is a seven-chest drawer made from fine oak. Lying down, it is hard to believe that she is nine years old. She looks much younger.

'Let me introduce you to Aisha,' Laura tells Dimple.

'Hi, Aisha,' Dimple says, smiling brightly. 'My name is Dimple. I am doing some work experience in the hospital for a week.'

Aisha gives them a shy smile.

'How are you feeling today?' Laura asks.

Aisha does not answer. She continues smiling, clutching her teddy bear close to her chest.

'I have a teddy bear, too,' Dimple says. 'Her name is Ellie. What is your teddy's name?'

Instead of responding, Aisha hides her face behind her teddy bear.

Laura brushes Aisha's teeth with a Barbie toothbrush.

'Will it hurt Aisha's mouth as she is not feeling well?' Dimple asks.

'Not at all,' Laura reassures her student. 'The bristle is soft.'

'Do patients shower every day?'

'Most patients have a full shower once a week, but the rest of the days, the nursing assistants will wipe their faces and bodies with a face flannel like this.' Next, Laura checks and records Aisha's temperature and blood pressure on the portable vital observation machine. She gets her iPad out to read the night nurse's observations for the medication required. 'These are Aisha's baseline measures.'

Dimple scratches her head, confused.

'In simple terms, we monitor her readings against this measure and act quickly if it goes below this mark.'

They are heading to the next room when Aisha's mum encounters them at the door and introduces herself. Laura gives her a brief update on her daughter's treatment plans.

'If you have any more questions, please come and look for me.'

'You can take a short break now, Dimple.'

'Thank you.'

Dimple goes to the staff room and picks up her phone from her locker.

'Hello, Nana.'

'Hello love, how is your day going?'

'Laura has shown me how to do the patients' personal care and monitor the baseline measures.' Dimple answers.

'That's a good lesson to learn, dear.'

'See you soon, Nana.'

'Bye, dear.'

CHAPTER 10

>❀<

Annual Family Barbecue

Mum and Dad are in the living room listening to the 10 o'clock news. The weather lady is giving the forecast for the next few days.

'Gloria, did you hear that?' Dad says. 'The weather should be fine this weekend.'

'That's great news!' Mum replies. 'Do you have anything in mind?'

'I think we should hold our family barbecue on Saturday so we can rest on Sunday before work on Monday.'

'I have a night shift on Sunday,' Mum says. 'But it should be fine. The children have been asking when the barbecue will be this year.'

✽ ✽ ✽ ✽ ✽ ✽ ✽ ✽

It is a dry, warm, humid Saturday evening in the Robinson household. Gloria is expecting her sister Nadia and the boys for a barbecue. It is nothing special; it is just a meet-up on that rare occasion when everyone is available, and it has gradually turned into an annual event. Since the children can invite their friends, Iryna's mum drops her off around noon.

The conservatory leads from the living room to the garden, where Dad has positioned a barbecue burner at one end. The conservatory takes up a sizeable chunk of the block-paved garden. Dad has assembled a small shed in a corner for his gardening furniture and bits of household equipment. Dimple and Mum put out some chairs and tables.

The doorbell rings, and Adam goes to open the front door. His cousins, David, Samuel, and Michael, catch him off guard with their usual fist bumps, and he struggles to stay on his feet.

'Boys!' Nadia yells, 'Show your cousin some respect. How many times have I told you to be civil when you are outside the house?'

'It's nothing, Aunty.' Adam says. 'We're all cool. How are you guys?'

Samuel says hi. They enter the house and stroll past the living room into the garden.

'Hi, boys,' Mum says before turning to her sister. 'Nadia, you must be proud of these young men. I see Samuel now has his hair in plaits like the other two. How old is Michael going to be this year?'

'Sixteen! Can you believe the baby of the house is sixteen?'

'Hello, Aunty,' Each boy returns to kiss Gloria on the cheek, and Michael gives her a warm hug.

'That's more like it,' she says, smiling and embracing her nephew fondly.

'Hi guys!' Dimple comes out from the kitchen, carrying some plates on a tray. She loves it when her cousins visit, especially at the same time. 'Meet my friend Iryna. She is new to our school and lives around the corner.'

Iryna looks at the boys shyly. Nadia's boys nod at her before heading for the barbecue burner, where Dad is.

'What are we eating today, Uncle?' Samuel asks.

Aunty Nadia follows them. 'You would think I don't feed them at home.' She feigns a cross face but loves it whenever her boys meet up with their cousins. 'Family is all that matters,' she and Gloria say together. 'The children will develop strong bonds as they grow up together.'

'We are family …. I've got all my cousins with me!' All the children click their fingers, wiggle their heads and dance around the garden.

Just then, Nana arrives. 'Hello everyone, it's been ages! Nadia, what on earth are you feeding these boys? They seem to shoot up like bamboo trees whenever I see them!'

'How are you, Nana?' Nadia holds her hands out to steady Nana on her feet.

Behind Nana, Dimple and Mum bring out the salad and other side dishes and place them on a table.

'Today,' Dad starts, 'we're having burgers, sausages, chicken drumsticks, pork chops, ribs, and steaks! We got some great deals thanks to Nadia's staff discount at her supermarket. Eat and enjoy yourselves, everyone.'

'We also brought some grilled gizzard and plantain,' Nadia adds.

'Are your friends coming over?' Nana asks Dimple.

Just then, the front doorbell rings. Dimple rushes to the door. Amara's mum volunteered to chauffeur and chaperone

Amara, Zainab, Natalie, and her new friend Sophia. They all follow Dimple to the garden.

'Adam, have you invited your friends, too?' Aunty Nadia asks.

'No, Aunty. They are busy today.'

Aunty Nadia picks up some sausages and starts handing them around.

'It's just as well…' Dimple declares. 'More food for me and my friends!'

They all settle down around the table, ready to eat. Adam has brought Nana's favourite armchair into the garden. Once they've collected their food, Dimple introduces her friends to one another.

'Iryna, meet Amara, Natalie, and Zainab from my primary school. Girls, Sophia and Iryna attend my new school. Iryna lives nearby.'

The girls exchange smiles and sit together in a corner of the garden where Dimple has placed two bean bags and some chairs.

'What are your favourite subjects at school?' Dimple asks her friends.

'I like chemistry,' Amara says.

'History,' Sophia chimes in.

'My favourite subjects are English and Sciences,' Dimple says.

'Mine is Arts,' Zainab says.

Smiling, Dimple nods at Natalie. 'We all know Natalie loves Maths!'

'Yes, Maths is my favourite subject,' Natalie says. 'I especially love algebra.'

'I wrote an essay about what I want to do after my GCSEs,' Dimple adds. 'It's my dream to be a nurse, like Mum.'

Overhearing their conversation, Dad draws Samuel and Michael's attention. 'What do you boys want to do when you leave school?'

'They want to be professional footballers,' Aunty Nadia replies. 'I keep telling them to have a plan 'B', as not everyone can be a professional footballer.'

'It's all these things they see on social media,' Nana remarks. 'Footballers with their flashy cars, glamorous women around them....'

'They are called 'WAGS', Nana,' Mum interjects, 'Wives and Girlfriends.'

'And their wages are obscene,' Dad adds. 'They don't know what to do with their money.'

Nana clears her throat. 'You must admit there are some talents among the footballers. The other day, I watched Lamine Yamal, the 16-year-old Spanish wonder kid, lighting up Euro 2024. What a joy!'

'I cannot believe Nana just said that!' David says. Laughter erupts from everyone at the thought of Nana watching the match.

'Football is not just for men, you know,' Nana retorts. 'I love watching the international games.'

David is licking his lips, clearly enjoying his burger and chips.

'This grilled gizzard and plantain is as tasty as ever, Nadia,' Nana says between mouthfuls. 'I think you should teach Dimple how to make them so she can make them for me occasionally.'

Headphones on, Samuel leisurely picks at his chicken drumsticks and sweetcorn. 'Lamine is only a year older than Michael,' he remarks.

'What's that supposed to mean?' Michael snaps.

A smiling Samuel raises his arms in self-defence, stepping back from his unusually belligerent brother.

Michael waves a fist. 'He is a talented footballer, and he has several years of playing football ahead.'

'My favourite tournament goal was Jude Bellingham's left-foot goal.' Dad puts in.

'Pure genius!' Adam leaps up from his chair and starts a running commentary. 'England had eighty-six seconds to spare them from an embarrassing defeat against Slovakia, and then came Jude Bellingham! In a flash of genius, as his left leg kicked an imaginary football, Bellingham took off in a confident show of athleticism and individual skill to send a stunning overhead kick past Slovakian keeper Martin Dubravka!'

All the boys shout an animated, 'Goal!'

'Okay, boys, no more football stories!' Dimple interjects, irritated by the conversation. 'When I get married, my husband will not be allowed to watch football all the time like Adam.'

'Good luck with that, Dimple,' Mum says knowingly. 'Is that another dream of yours?'

'Mum, you should not encourage Adam and the boys to always talk about football! It's so annoyingly boring.'

'My dream is to become a lawyer when I finish school,' Iryna says. 'Then I can send all the corrupt politicians to jail. I may also have to run for President in my country to accomplish that.'

Dimple winks at her friend. 'Vote Iryna for President!'

'Why not?' Mum remarks. 'Kamala Harris is the Democrats' presidential nominee in the US. If she wins, she becomes the first Asian and first woman President of the United States.'

Nana, who has nodded off after happily enjoying her grilled gizzard, sits up. 'I have a dream... 'that I will be surrounded by my great-grandchildren, and we will go on big adventures.'

Mum starts laughing. 'You have a while to fulfil that dream!'

Adam and Dimple exchange looks before bursting into fits of laughter.

'Who remembers 'The Dream' of American basketball in the 1980s and 90s?' Mum continues.

'Ha! I do.' Dad says. 'Hakeem the Dream'.

Born in Lagos, Nigeria, Hakeem Abdul Olajuwon is a retired professional basketball player. Considered one of basketball's all-time greats, he was nicknamed **"The Dream"** after repeatedly dunking so effortlessly that his college coach said it "looked like a dream." He played as a Centre in the NBA for the Houston Rockets and the Toronto Raptors.

'How about playing basketball instead of football, David?' Nana asks.

'No way!' David blurts out.

The children chuckle at the suggestion. 'That is so not cool,' Michael says.

'It worked for Hakeem,' Nana argues.

'But you always tell us to follow our passion, Nana,' Samuel points out.

Adam goes indoors, returns with his laptop, and starts playing music. Everyone moves cheerfully to the beat. Mum brings out the dessert and cuts it into small portions, which she dishes nicely into dessert bowls. Dimple places the bowls on a tray and takes them around for each guest.

'This cake is lovely,' Adam says, taking a big bite into his mouth at once.

'Why don't we discuss Nana's upcoming birthday?' Mum whispers to Nadia, and the two head for the living room.

'Who has heard of the brat dance?' Zainab asks the girls.

Iryna shakes her head. 'Not me,'

Zainab enlightens her friends - *The Brat Girl* album is by Charli XCX

'*It's brat. You're brat, That's brat.*'

'I saw Charli XCX doing the brat dance on TikTok. It's super cool!' Zainab says, attempting the moves:

Left arm. Right arm. Chest. 4 taps. 3 hip taps. Corner. Hands up. Split down 4x. Cross face. Head shake[1].

The girls try to copy Zainab's movements.

Dimple is jiggling about, stumbling, and crashing into Sophia as she dances. 'We're having a brat summer, after all!' she says.

---

[1] Note: https://www.tiktok.com/@charlixcxon

CHAPTER 11

➤✿❮

To Party or Not to Party, That is the Question

At noon on the Sunday after the barbecue, Mum flips through the TV channels in the living room.

'Hey, I was watching that!' Dad says from his position on the big settee.

'James, you keep rewatching quiz programmes you have recorded over the weeks.

'But I was here first,' Dad moans.

'And I live here too!' Mum says, 'I want to watch something else.'

'Fine. What did you and Nadia decide for Nana's surprise party?'

'James, you can't surprise Nana with her ears behind the walls. She sees and hears everything going on around her. She even walked in on our conversation yesterday!'

Dad laughs. 'That's true. I guess the bubble has burst, then?'

Nana walks in. 'I heard voices and thought the children were fighting over TV channels again. I never imagined it was the adults!'

'Nana, your son needs to grow up! He watches repeat quiz programmes all the time.'

'I'm hardly at home to watch the telly anyway,' Dad says. 'You should indulge me now and then.'

'We want to watch *Rich Holiday, Poor Holiday*,' Mum says, winking at Nana.

'That was a good gathering yesterday,' Nana says.

'Yeah, we were fortunate that the weather was good,' Dad replies.

'I heard you talking earlier. I really don't want any fuss on my birthday this year,' Nana says.

'Oh, it's no worry at all,' Mum says, 'Your 70th is an important milestone. It's neither unnecessary nor a fuss, Nana.

You celebrate others, so it is your turn to be celebrated. Plus, you do special things for your friends on their birthdays.

'I'm sure Dad would want you to celebrate this milestone,' Dad adds.

'I miss your dad more when discussing my birthday.'

'He will be looking down on you with pride and affection,' Dad says. 'Remember the 70th birthday party surprise you organised for Mable at your club? She still talks about the party, one year on.'

Mum picks up her phone to make a call. 'Hey, Nadia! You mentioned yesterday that you have a good new caterer?'

'Yes, she catered for my friend's party, and everyone was impressed. The menu was good, and the food was tasty. I will get her details for you. Has Nana agreed to a party?'

'We're still trying to convince her,' Mum replies. 'Let me put you on speakerphone.'

'Nana, please, we want a party, we want to dance and celebrate you!' Nadia wheedles.

'To party or not to party, Nana,' Dad murmurs. 'That is the question.'

'Alright then, you all are so good to me,' Nana concedes. 'Nothing over the top, though, just a small one with my family and close friends.'

Nadia can be heard chuckling over the phone. 'Sure, Nana! We're going to have a party. I will contact Nessa to discuss cake options and, to remove the stress of planning, let's hire my favourite event planner, Bimpy, aka 'Adorned for you', to organise the party and decorate the hall. She can work closely with the caterer.'

'I will start writing up a guest list,' Mum says.

'I will contact Nana's friends in Scotland,' Dad says. 'I can also take Adam, David and his brothers to buy the drinks.'

'I have several theme ideas for the party,' Mum says.

Dad grabs the remote control from her. 'Why don't you continue the conversation in Nana's room?'

'Just because you want to get back to your old quiz programmes,' Mum teases. 'Nadia, stay on the line. Nana and I are moving to her room.'

'So, what are we going to wear?' Nadia asks excitedly.

'Peace at last!' Dad says under his breath.

Mum sits down at Nana's table. 'Like I was saying, Nana, we must book your hair appointment with Jade.'

'Is she back at work?' Nana asks.

'Not yet, but she will come here to do your hair.'

'Oh, that would allow me to see her little one!'

'Apparently, Helena makes good dresses.'

Nadia laughs out loud. 'Not for this party. We are wearing the best of the best to Nana's 70th!

'How can we involve Helena in the party arrangements, then?'

'I will think of something for her to do.'

'That would be lovely,' Nana says.

➤✿❧

CHAPTER 12

Summer Festival at the Hospital

It is the annual summer festival at the hospital where Mum works. Mum and Rita, her colleague, have been working hard since last year planning the event.

'Gloria, will Dimple be helping us this year?' Rita asks.

'She is coming with her school team as an observer, this year.'

'However, Nana is coming along, to help Mable at her stall.'

'We're the Ace team!' Rita says. 'Plus, this year's festival will be even better than previous ones.

'I hope we raise more funds for the hospital this year,' Mum adds.

❋ ❋ ❋ ❋ ❋ ❋ ❋ ❋

There have been many activities from the start of the week.

On Wednesday, Adam came with Jay and Ollie to a football match between Rainbow Ward (in orange jerseys with white shorts) and Hope Ward (in blue and white-striped jerseys with white shorts).

Friday is the final day. Rita, Gloria, and the other staff have arranged lots of activities. The maintenance team secures two white tents in the main garden, with room for a music deck.

Mr Phillip brought the science students, dressed in their school uniforms, to the hospital to experience the summer festival. Dimple walks around the grounds with Jane, Sophia, Iryna, and Tamara. She examines the pictures of uniformed nurses hanging on big posters, showing their roles and responsibilities.

'Look, Sophia, here is Florence Nightingale!'

'And over here at the back is Mary Seacole,' Iryna announces from behind the poster.

The students attend a workshop in one of the large halls, where Mum leads a session on the history of the hospital and choosing nursing as a career.

Ward nurse Agnes brings her seven-year-old daughter to the Karaoke session. Little Naomi picks up the microphone and belts out *Barbie Girl* by Aqua, a Danish-Norwegian dance-pop group.

The crowd applauds when she takes a bow, and her proud mum leads Naomi to the ice cream van. They join the queue of staff, visitors and other guests, and Agnes orders a banana ice lolly for herself and an ice cream cone with chocolate syrup for Naomi. The staff take turns on the karaoke machine, singing and dancing to ABBA songs including *Dancing Queen*.

A yellow American-style Type B School bus is parked elsewhere in the garden. The single-deck bus has a step entry, and on the door is a black tablet with white lettering listing the different available sessions (Swedish, Thai, and deep tissue massages included) that staff members can book. This free service is only open to staff, providing a much-needed break and reminder not to neglect their health while looking after patients.

- Sports massage.
- Reflexology
- Deep tissue massage
- Balbcare treatment

Susan arrives for her noon massage. She is having the Balbcare treatment, a luxury waterless manicure and pedicure that only takes a few minutes and locks in 100% more moisture than similar water-based treatments.

❅ ❅ ❅ ❅ ❅ ❅ ❅ ❅

Mable sits under a green outdoor parasol, shading her from the sun. For weeks, she has knitted woollen baby socks, baby and adult shawls, gloves of assorted colours and shapes, teapot covers and table coasters and has pledged all the proceeds to the hospital. Nana helps her to organise the stall into a pretty display. She puts the items out, and Mable puts price stickers on them.

'We make a good team, don't we, Mable?'

'Yes, Pat, we are the dream team!' Mable replies.

Dimple and her group walk up to Mable's stall.

'Hello Nana, Aunty Mable.'

'How is your day going with your friends,' Nana asks.

'Interesting, we have been making notes as we go along.' Dimple picks up a cute, knitted poodle sweater. 'I love this one for Kitty!' She starts talking to Kitty, who is beside Nana. 'Hey Kitty, do you like this grey sweater?'

Kitty wags her tail and sticks her tongue out.

'I'll take that as a 'Yes', then.' Dimple gets her little wallet out. 'Mable, can I buy this, please?'

'Sure, but you get a discount as my favourite person,' Mable replies.

'I will pay for you, Dimple,' Nana says.

'Thank you, Nana; see you at home, Kitty.'

A lady picks up a pink shawl and a pair of baby boots. Nana bags the items, collects the payment and extracts some change from her canvas bumbag, which she hands over with the bag.

The woman walks away from the stall with a 'Thank you, ma'am.'

The students are having fun getting to know the other guests and scribbling their experiences at the event in their little notebooks.

Aunty Nadia is painting *Rainbows, Hello Kitty, Spiderman*, and other images on the little ones' faces using a non-toxic, easily removed paint. The happy kids run off excitedly to show their parents the result. *Waterloo*, *Dancing Queen,* and other ABBA songs are coming from the garden tent.

Finally, the CEO takes to the stage with the microphone.

'Thank you all for your support during our summer festival and the different activities since Monday. You would have seen some students in uniform taking notes throughout the day. I hope we have inspired them to follow their dreams and that they will one day work in some capacity at this hospital.

Please continue to enjoy yourselves, and we look forward to seeing you all at next year's summer festival.'

CHAPTER 13

> ✿ ❮

Sip and Paint Class

Nana is lying on her double bed, dialling a number on her mobile phone. She is wearing a grey tracksuit with a grey hooded top.

'Hello, is that Jocelyn?'

'Yes, whom am I speaking with, please?'

'It's Patricia, Dimple's Nana, how are you?'

'I'm good, thank you.'

'I was wondering if you would like to attend a Sip and Paint session at the over 60's club tomorrow. The session is open to all ages, and as it is a family event, Iryna can come with Dimple.'

'That is marvellous! Fred has a prior engagement, but I can accompany Iryna and Helena. Is it free?'

'I'm afraid not because of the materials involved. There is a concession for club members, however. Don't worry, James will pay for all of us if you can come.'

'Hold on, Helena just entered the room.' (from the muffled sound, Jocelyn has covered the mouthpiece) but Nana can still hear the conversation.

'Helena, are you free tomorrow afternoon? The Robinsons are inviting us to a painting workshop.'

'What time?'

'2pm,' Nana confirms.

Jocelyn relays this to Helena. 'Pat, that is fine. We will meet you there at two o'clock. Helena pointed out the building to us on the way home from the school last week.'

'It's a date then. See you tomorrow. I'm sure Dimple will be happy when I tell her.' Nana says.

'So will Iryna. It will help them relax and do something besides schoolwork.'

'You're right. Dimple has had a lot of homework recently. See you all tomorrow,' Nana concludes.

'Bye, Patricia.' Jocelyn sends her love to Gloria and the rest of the family, and they hang up. Almost immediately, there is a knock on Nana's door.

'Who is it?'

Dimple walks in without answering.

'Hello, young lady! I didn't hear the front door. How was school today?'

'Thank God it's Friday, Nana.' Dimple slumps on the chair by Nana's reading table. 'School was okay, but I am tired. It's been a busy week. I came home on the bus with Iryna and Sophia. What have you been up to today?'

'Not much, dear. I had a good rest, but I have a good surprise for you.'

Dimple sits up abruptly. 'What surprise, Nana?'

'I have just been speaking with Jocelyn. There is a Sip and Paint event at my club tomorrow afternoon, and I asked if she would like to come.'

'That's great, Nana! I'm sure it will be fun for you.'

'Since it's a family event, you can attend with Iryna. Jocelyn says they can make it.'

Dimple gets her phone out of her school bag. 'Even better! I will call Iryna now.'

'Why don't you take off your uniform first?'

'Alright, Nana. I'll be right back.'

Dimple talks to Iryna as she walks through the kitchen and living room. As she climbs the stairs, Kitty strolls down to welcome her.

'Hi Kitty,' Dimple bends down to stroke her ears. 'Have you been a good girl with Nana today?'

Kitty wags her tongue, and they go up the stairs together. Still talking to Iryna, Dimple dumps her school bag on the floor.

'Yes, it's tomorrow. Nana says you are coming with your Mum and Jocelyn.'

'I'm looking forward to that,' Iryna replies.

'Super, see you then!' Dimple puts her phone away. 'Did you hear that, Kitty? We are all going to do some painting at Nana's club tomorrow. I'm sure we can get a little brush for you to paint with, too!'

❋ ❋ ❋ ❋ ❋ ❋ ❋ ❋

The next morning, Dimple heads to Nana's bedroom wearing her silk lilac pyjamas with Kitty in her arms. She treads softly into the room.

'Nana? Are you awake?'

'Yes, love. How are you this morning?' Nana pushes back the duvet so she can sit up.

Dimple walks over to open the blinds.

'Thank you, pet. Did you sleep well?'

'Yes, Nana. I was thinking that we don't have the materials for today's painting session.'

'John ordered the materials to be delivered to his house. He will bring them with him.'

'I promised Kitty that I would get her a small paintbrush.'

'I'm sure that won't be a problem,' Nana assures her granddaughter.

'Do you mind If I do my homework in your room? Adam is playing loud music in his room again.'

'Sure, love. Can I help?'

'I just need to read two chapters from my textbook for next week's English Literature class.'

Nana gets up and walks to her wardrobe. 'Let me check what I can wear this afternoon.'

'Nana, my other friends are not talking to me because I am friends with Iryna,' Dimple says.

'What other friends?'

'Jane, Tamara, Sophia ….'

'Do you involve them when you spend time with Iryna?'

'Yes, but things have not been the same since we won the English essay competition.'

'Give it time but include them in your activities with Iryna.'

'I will. Thanks, Nana. I should read my second chapter tomorrow and prepare for this afternoon instead.'

'What do you think of this red shirt, Dimple?'

'Great choice, Nana! C'mon Kitty, let's get you ready to do some painting today.' Dimple packs her book into her bag and leaves the room.

She stops by her parents' room.

'Dad, Mum, who is attending the club with us today?'

'Your dad will drop you and Nana off,' Mum says. 'I will pick you up.'

'Have you done your homework, Dimple?'

'I started it in Nana's room. I will complete it tomorrow.'

'Take your dirty laundry downstairs so I can add it to this morning's wash,' Mum says.

Dimple heads for her room. 'I will do that now.'

❋ ❋ ❋ ❋ ❋ ❋ ❋ ❋

At noon, Dimple enters the living room wearing a brown jumper under her brown corduroy dungarees. In her arms is Kitty, dressed in a brown tartan coat.

'Nana, are you ready?' she calls out. 'We don't want Iryna to get to the club before us.' She gently puts Kitty down and nudges her. 'Go and see what Nana is doing.'

On cue, Kitty runs towards Nana's room.

Dad is in the living room. He is dressed in a black tracksuit, reading a magazine.

'Oh! I didn't realise you were down here, Dad.'

'I've been waiting here patiently for you ladies.'

Dimple gives her dad a peck on his forehead. 'That makes a nice change!'

Nana reaches the door, bends down and strokes Kitty's head. In a red long-sleeved shirt, a black sweater, and black trousers, she enters the kitchen and gets out a biscuit for Kitty.

Kitty happily runs towards Dimple with the biscuit in her mouth.

'You spoil her for me, Nana. Can you believe Dad is waiting for us, for a change?'

'Yes, I want to run some errands on the way back,' Dad replies. 'The earlier we leave, the quicker I can do what I need to.'

Nana, Dad, Dimple and Kitty head out to Dad's car. Nana sits in the back. 'How is Gloria?'

'She is resting.'

Dimple sits next to Dad. 'Thank you for paying for our painting session, Dad.'

Dad starts to drive. 'It's my pleasure. I'm sure you'll all have fun.'

'What about Adam?' Nana asks.

'Still in bed, as usual,' Dad says.

Nana changes the subject. 'The road is quiet at this time of the day.'

Dimple glances out of the window. 'Most people who don't have to be at work are probably having a lie-in before starting their Saturday routine.'

'Is Fred joining you today?'

'No, Dad, he is not coming.'

'An all-women affair, then?'

'John will be there,' Nana says.

Dad drives into the club's parking lot and gets out to open Nana's door. Dimple jumps out with Kitty in tow.

Kitty leads the group through the main door into the building. The brick bungalow has been given a fresh lick of red paint. John is arranging the main hall for the Sip and Paint event.

Dad greets him, and they shake hands.

'How have you been, James? Thanks for bringing the ladies over.'

'My pleasure,' Dad replies. 'Who is this young man?'

'Joshua, my 16-year-old nephew. He is visiting from Atlanta, where his parents live.'

'Hi,' Joshua says, nodding. He is wearing a black tracksuit over a white pair of trainers.

The easels are arranged in a circle around a main table, and there is a canvas for each person. Another canvas and easel at the head of the table are covered with a white cloth.

Dad hugs Nana, Dimple waves goodbye, and he leaves the hall.

'I will give you a hand with setting up,' Dimple tells the two men. She runs her fingers over the cloth. 'I wonder what is behind this?'

'No, Miss.' John says. 'No one is allowed to see that until everyone is here.'

'Hmm… That must be the master drawing,' Dimple tells Kitty.

Iryna enters the hall in blue jeans, dungarees, and a white T-shirt. 'Hi Dimple.'

'Hello Jocelyn,' Nana says. 'John, come and meet Iryna's family. Iryna is Dimple's new friend at school.'

'Hello, ladies,' John shakes hands with each of them. 'My name is John.'

Dimple grabs her friend by the arm. 'Iryna, will you help me put the paintbrushes on the table?'

'Sure, let's get started!'

'What's that behind the cloth?' Jocelyn asks.

'That's the master drawing. We're not allowed to see it yet,' Dimple says, moving around the tables, putting paint brushes, aprons, paint pots, pallets, and other items for each guest.

'What can we do to help?' Helena asks.

Nana points to an area in the hall. 'Set the food on the table in the corner.'

Soon, other guests start entering the hall.

'Pat!' Mable walks across the room, waving to her friend.

'Hello, Mable,' Nana says. 'Meet Helena, Jocelyn and Iryna.'

'Iryna, it's good to meet you at last!' Mable says. 'Patricia has told me a lot about you.'

'We are about to start now, everyone. Please take your seats,' John announces. 'I will show you the master drawing now. Dimple, help me remove the cloth. Drum roll, please.'

The guests enthusiastically knock on the table as Dimple gently takes the cloth off the canvas.

'Wow, it is a dazzling picture of the night sky with the moon and stars!' she exclaims.

There is a round of applause from everyone.

'Let's get started,' Nana says eagerly.

Soft music fills the room, and the guests immerse themselves in the task. Dimple puts Kitty's paintbrush between her paws.

'Hey, Kitty, look at me,' Iryna says, taking Kitty's picture on her smartphone.

'Thank you, Iryna. It did not even cross my mind to take a picture. She is cute in her apron and with her brush, isn't she?'

'She sure is,' Iryna replies as she sits beside Dimple – Mable is to Dimple's left – and begins her painting. John sits between Nana and Helena while Jocelyn starts a conversation with Rhona. The other guests chat casually, getting to know each other.

'Your nan tells me you did some work experience recently,' Mable says to Dimple, brushing away on her canvas. 'How was it?'

'I was nervous on the first day but gradually overcame my fears. I learned how to take blood pressure readings and patient temperatures and use different types of equipment.'

'Your nan promised you would come over to do some basic health checks for me.'

'She told me. I will come soon, Aunt Mable.'

John claps briskly to draw the group's attention. 'Right. It's time for a break. Please come to the table for some nibbles and drinks.'

Dimple, Iryna, and Kitty walk to the round table, where various crisps, sandwiches, olives, and fruits are on display.

'Over here for wine,' John waves to those with food on their plates. He has put on a white cotton apron and acts as a butler. Joshua helps by bringing more supplies from the kitchen as needed.

'Red or white wine?'

'Red for me, please,' Nana says.

Jocelyn is nodding. 'I will have red wine, too,'

'White wine for me, please, 'Dimple says cheekily.

'You must be joking, Miss, 'John retorts. 'Orange or apple juice, which would you like?'

Dimple flashes her dimple. 'Orange juice, please.'

John hands her a glass. 'You are yet to introduce your friend to me, Dimple.'

'Her name is Iryna. We are in the same class at school.'

'Well, Miss Iryna, orange or apple juice?'

Iryna smiles. 'Can I have some apple juice, please?'

'Here you go, ma'am,' and Iryna smiles again.

'And you are?' John asks Helena.

'Helena, I'm Iryna's mum. A glass of white wine, please?'

John takes a wine bottle from the ice bucket. 'Coming right up! You can take your food back to your tables but try to avoid spillages so we don't slip over food or liquid. Thank you.'

'This painting is much clearer after a cold glass of wine,' Helena remarks to Jocelyn with a chuckle.

'I quite agree with you,' Jocelyn says merrily. 'The brush is going over the canvas more smoothly.'

'Haha!' Nana chortles across the table. 'You ladies are seeing double after one glass of wine.'

Dimple and Iryna exchange glances and burst out laughing at the adults.

'What do you do for work?' Rhona asks Jocelyn.

'I run an after-school club with my husband. Fred and I are both retired.'

'How do you find that? Is it tiring at your age?'

'It can be demanding work chasing after misbehaving children and waiting for working parents who pick up their children late. A young lady helps occasionally, but the team is small to keep costs down.'

John walks around, looking at each canvas. 'How's the painting going, everyone?'

Nana raises her half-empty glass of wine.

'Cheers, Patricia! I hope the painting is going well.' he says with a smile. 'Ladies and gentlemen, when you're done, put your signature at the bottom and leave your painting on the table to my left.'

'I'm done!' Iryna announces before taking her canvas to the table.

'That looks very pretty,' Nana says. 'Well done, Iryna.'

The ten guests take their paintings to the table one by one. Then, Nana walks up to the piano in the corner and runs her fingers over the keys.

> *'They can come true*
> *They can come true*
> *Move a step closer....'*

'Oh, that song is 'Dreams, by Gabrielle,' Rhona declares, rising to her feet.

Jocelyn gets up. 'I love her distinctive voice.' They both start moving to the music.

'While you are dancing, Josh will help me to judge the best painting,' John says.

Joshua goes up to the table and starts scrutinising one picture after another.

'Pick your best three and put them here,' John nods to the right.

'These two are tops,' Josh says thoughtfully. 'But I can't decide about the 3rd one.'

'I agree with those two; perhaps this one is in third place?'

Josh nods. 'Sounds good.'

Nana finishes her piece, everyone claps, and she stands up and takes a bow.

'If you are ready for the results, please take your seats,' John says.

'In 3rd place is this painting by Mable.' (clap clap clap)

'In 2nd place is Patricia!' (clap clap clap)

'And in 1st place is…Dimple! Dimple, can you tell us a bit about your painting?'

Dimple gets up. 'Well, the darkness in the background represents nighttime,' she shyly explains, 'which is when I dream of the future. The moon shows creativity, while the stars represent my friends and family, who surround me as I work towards my dream.'

'Oh, that was a good speech, even if I am biased towards my granddaughter,' Nana says to Mable proudly.

CHAPTER 14

> ✣ <

Happy Birthday, Nana

The time is 8 am. Dimple is still in her pyjamas as she rushes to Nana's bedroom and gives her a big hug and kiss. 'Happy birthday, Nana!'

'Thank you, darling.'

Today is Nana's 70th birthday.

Dad and Mum enter Nana's room. 'Where's the birthday girl?' Dad says, handing a wrapped gift to Nana. 'Happy birthday, Mum.'

Mum presents Nana with a bouquet of fresh flowers and a kiss on both cheeks. 'Happy birthday Nana.'

Dad starts humming a tune, grabs Mum's hand and leads her in a ballroom dance. 'We Robinsons have the X-Factor, and we put the glitz into any party!'

'Da-ad, please stop being funny!' Dimple groans, shaking her head.

Dad hired the local Community Leisure Centre, while Aunty Nadia ordered food from Laraba caterers and two birthday cakes from NESSENCE Cakes.

✽ ✽ ✽ ✽ ✽ ✽ ✽ ✽

The thirty-year-old Community Leisure Centre is a white building on two floors. The first floor has a gym and a nail studio, and the party hall is on the ground floor. As you enter the building, a reception desk is to your left. The entrance is decorated in silver, gold and black. The deejay, a jolly-looking man wearing headphones, has set up his deck and instruments on the stage and is now getting ready, doing microphone checks and other bits.

The high table is set up in front, with three chairs for Nana, Dad, and Mum. To the right, another table with Nana's cakes, birthday cards, and decorations. The tables are arranged in circles, each with a fresh bouquet of gold and lilac flowers on a white tablecloth that drapes to the floor. The chairs have white cover sheets with lilac ribbons tied at the back. Finger snacks—nuts, canapes, and a jug of water—have been placed on each table. Gold petals are strewn across the tables, with white, neatly folded cotton napkins and silver table runners completing the décor. Mum and Aunty Nadia work with Bimpy to correctly place the guests' names.

The first set of guests start arriving, led by John and Rhona from the over 60's club. After greeting Mum, they locate their names on the table plan by the door before taking their seats. Music floats in the background as others make their way in, including Franklin and Mable. They greet one another before sitting behind John and Rhona.

Nana walks in on Dad's arm, looking beautiful in her long, silver evening gown. Her hair is a sophisticated take on the topknot. The high bun is pure class. The guests treat her to a standing ovation. Dad escorts Nana to her seat on the high table. He sits on her right, and Mum is on her left. Aunty Nadia, Iryna's mum, Fred and Jocelyn are at a table nearby. Adam's friends are at a separate table, as are Dimple and her friends.

'Hey, Dimple – look behind you,' Iryna says.

'What?' Dimple turns toward the door to see Tamara, Jane and Sophia coming in with Tamara's mum as their chaperone.

'Who invited them?'

Nana smiles knowingly from her position on the high table.

Mum approaches the new arrivals. 'Thank you for bringing the girls.'

'Thank you for having us,' Tamara's mum replies.

'Nana insisted on inviting your friends, Dimple.'

'You kept that a secret from me all this time, Mum! Adam, were you aware of this?' She bellows across the room.

'Not guilty – that's all I'm saying.' Adam replies, turning in the other direction.

Mum ushers them to a table. 'Please sit down and share this special moment with our family.'

'Iryna and I will join you,' Dimple says.

'Sorry for giving you a hard time at school, Dimple,' Tamara says, looking apologetic.

'The same goes for Iryna,' Jane adds.

'Girls, you have made today extra special for me. Thank you.' Dimple says, feeling a little emotional.

Dad gets up to propose a toast. 'Please raise your glasses to this wonderful woman, my mother, Mrs Patricia Robinson. Mum, thank you for all you continue to do for me and our family.'

Bimpy invites Nana to the cake table. 'At the count of three, Nana will cut her cake… one, two, three!'

'Cheers!' everyone shouts as Nana slices her cake.

The photographer invites guests from each table to take photographs with Nana, starting with her immediate family. All the while, the stewards in white coats move briskly from one table to the next, serving dinner.

Nana rises to make her speech. 'I am blessed to have my friends and family share this wonderful day with me. Thank you all for your lovely gifts. My birthday is incredibly special because everyone here demonstrates how much they love me. I honour the memory of my late husband, and I am proud of James, my son, who has looked after me since I lost my husband. His wife, Gloria, is the daughter I have always wished for. My grandchildren, Adam and Dimple, are my pride and joy. Once again, please accept my heartfelt thanks and gratitude.'

As the guests clap, the lights go dim.

What could be happening? Dimple wonders, looking around to find out. The guests can be heard whispering in the silence.

David, Samuel, and Michael, the saxophone trio, walk up slowly from the back of the room, playing Happy Birthday. They stop in front of Nana, and the lights come on again. Nana is overwhelmed. Tears of joy are in her eyes as she reaches for her handkerchief in her silver clutch bag. Dabbing her eyes with it, she makes little sounds as she looks around at her seated guests, taking in her well-wishers' faces.

When the boys finish playing the tune, Dimple and Adam join them to lead everyone in singing *Happy Birthday*. The guests are on their feet as well. The children warmly embrace Nana in turns before returning to their seats.

'You have such a lovely family, Dimple,' Sophia says when Dimple rejoins them at their table.

Suddenly, Mable starts singing…

'For she's a jolly good fellow, and so, say all of us, Hurrah!'

Then, the moment everyone has patiently waited for arrives! Dance! Dance! Dance!

The DJ starts playing the Stevie Wonder song – *Isn't She Lovely*.

Dad has the first dance with Nana. Then John takes over, and Dad invites Mum to the dance floor. Everyone gets to their feet, and the dancing continues into the night.

'Have you enjoyed yourself tonight,' John asks as he dances with Nana.

'This party is truly special – El Sueno,' Nana replies with a twinkle as she dances in step with John.

Dimple is dancing with all her friends – Iryna, Jane, Tamara, and Sophia.

'No Brat dance tonight, girls,' Dimple says as she moves on the dance floor.

'It's just as well that Zainab is not here,' Iryna says.

They all burst out laughing.

'May all our dreams come true,' – Dimple whispers to her friends.

>❋<

I Am My Dream

It is 6am on Friday, and Dimple drives to work in her red Mini. Sporting thick, black-framed oval glasses, she checks the clock on her dashboard while tapping her fingers on the steering wheel.

There is an unusual queue outside the train station, and Dimple wonders what is happening. Switching from her usual channel to the news channel, she only hears the tail end of the report, which is something about how many services are affected globally today.

What could this mean?

She enters the hospital gates and drives towards the staff parking area, turning off the engine and removing the key from the ignition. With her backpack on her back and lunch bag in her left hand, she greets the hospital porter and takes the lift to her third-floor ward.

'I need a strong coffee to start my shift today,' she mutters in the female changing room.

'Morning, Kelly,' she says to her colleague. 'I'm going downstairs for coffee. Do you need anything from the canteen?'

'A cappuccino, please. I will give you the money when you get back.'

Dimple changes into her blue uniform and locks her clothes in her locker.

'No worries, if anyone asks, let them know where I am.'

She takes the stairs down to the canteen and is greeted by a big sign in front of the cash counter:

'CASH ONLY'

'Can I have a large white coffee and a medium cappuccino, please.'

'Sure,' The lady at the end of the counter says. Her hair is covered with a black net, and a navy-blue apron is over her clothes.

'Why is this sign here?' Dimple asks as the lady prepares her order.

'All our card readers have failed this morning. Apologies for any inconvenience.'

'This is horrible! On a day like this at the end of the week, no one has any cash left!'

The news comes on from the television screen at the end of the room:

'A massive tech failure has caused travel chaos around the world, with banking and healthcare services also badly hit. Flights have been grounded because of the IT outage - a flaw which left many computers displaying blue error screens.

There were long queues, delays, and flight cancellations at airports around the world, as passengers had to be manually checked in.

Cyber-security firm CrowdStrike has admitted that the problem was caused by an update to its antivirus software, which is designed to protect Microsoft Windows devices from malicious attacks.

Microsoft has said it is taking "mitigation action" to deal with "the lingering impact" of the outage.'

-- BBC News 19 July 2024

'I have no money in my wallet. I came with my bank card.'

The barista smiles. 'You can pay later. What's your name?'

Dimple points to her name badge. 'Dimple. I work at The Rainbow Unit on the children's ward.'

'No worries,' the lady adds her name to a growing list before handing over two cups in a brown cardboard cup holder.

'Thank you. I promise to come back and pay later this afternoon.' She takes the lift to the third floor and walks to the day room.

'Here you go, Kelly.' She gives Kelly the cup inscribed with 'C' for cappuccino. 'I couldn't pay for our coffees because the system was down and would not accept my card, and I had no cash. Microsoft's systems apparently shut down after a software update error from a US security firm.'

'Yes,' Kelly replies. 'The NHS login is also experiencing problems when I click on it through the app.'

Dimple sips her white coffee. 'Great! Today can only get better. The entire world has shut down.'

'Laura says Jack is your first patient for the day.'

'Thank you. I will start my day with young Jack as soon as I finish my drink.'

Other staff members mill around the day room, discussing the IT outage. Dimple puts her empty cup in the green recycle bin, rubs her hands over the top of her shirt, and straightens her uniform before heading to Jack's room. At the room's entrance, she cuts off a white disposable apron from a roll, puts it on, and ties the ribbon behind her back.

'Hello, my name is Dimple, and I am your nurse today. What's your name?'

'Jack,' the twelve-year-old replies, consciously shifting his legs on his hospital bed. His curly strawberry-coloured hair is unbrushed, and he tries to keep his hair in place, away from his eyes.

Dimple takes two medium-sized gloves out of a box and puts them on. 'Hi Jack, how are you feeling today?'

'Alright.'

She removes the red folder at the end of Jack's bed. 'Our computer system is down today,' she says, flicking through the folder's latest entry. She adjusts her glasses to sit properly on the bridge of her nose. 'I see your stats are a little below the baseline.'

She goes to the corner, drags a trolley to the bedside, picks up an Infrared Thermometer and points it at Jack's forehead.

'38.6 degrees; that is rather high, Jack.' She plucks a pen out of her left breast pocket and records the reading on paper.

Jack is taking deep breaths all the while.

'Stretch your arm towards me.'

Jack stretches his left hand towards Dimple, who gently drapes the blood pressure machine cloth over his arm. With her stethoscope, she also checks for sounds as an aneroid gauge squeezes Jack's artery.

She waits for five minutes but cannot get a reading. 'Shall we try your other arm?'

Jack rolls up his blue pyjama sleeves and stretches his right hand to Dimple. She repeats the procedure and waits for the result.

'120/80 mmHg. That's good. Well done, Jack.'

He nods.

'I'll speak to the doctor about your fever. Have a good rest, I'll be back soon.'

It's going to be a tedious day without a working system, she thinks as she documents her actions, observations, and readings in a notebook.

Dimple goes in search of the doctor on duty.

'I am my Dream.'

ABOUT THE AUTHOR

> ❀ ‹

Bola Dada is the author of *Dimple Dares to Ask,* a book about the 2020 pandemic from an inquisitive twelve-year-old girl's perspective.

An Information Professional and Chartered Librarian, she currently works in Project Management, lives in London and has two adult children. Bola is a family-oriented avid reader who enjoys travelling. She is passionate about nurturing children to reach their full potential through reading.

Aimed at nine-to fourteen-year-olds, *Dimple Dares To Dream* is her second book.